Swim to Win

SWIM TO WIN

Training for Competition

Bernard Charles

FABER AND FABER
London   Boston

First published in 1979
by Faber and Faber Limited
3 Queen Square London WC1
Phototypeset in V.I.P. Palatino by
Western Printing Services Ltd, Bristol
Printed in Great Britain by
Redwood Burn Ltd, Trowbridge and Esher

All rights reserved

© *Bernard Charles, 1979*

CONDITIONS OF SALE
This book is sold subject to the condition that it shall not, by way of trade or otherwise, be lent, re-sold, hired out or otherwise circulated without the publisher's prior consent in any form of binding or cover other than that in which it is published and without a similar condition including this condition being imposed on the subsequent purchaser

British Library Cataloguing in Publication Data

Charles, Bernard
  Swim to win.
  1. Swimming
  I. Title
  792.2'1   GV837

  ISBN 0–571–11344–3
  ISBN 0–571–11401–6   Pbk

Contents

		page	
	Introduction		7
	Prologue		9
1.	*The Swimming Body*: Stamina and Endurance		11
2.	*The Swimming Body*: Strength		15
3.	*The Swimming Body*: Breathing and Variational Activities		23
4.	*The Swimming Body*: Mobility		25
5.	*The Swimming Body*: Power/Weight Ratio		32
6.	*The Swimming Body*: Diet		34
7.	*The Swimming Body*: Psychological		37
8.	*The Swimming Body*: The Swimming Strokes		39
9.	*The Swimming Training*: General		51
10.	*The Swimming Training*: Specific		58
11.	The Swimming Coach		76
12.	The Swimming Competition		82
13.	The Swimmer's Parents		86

Introduction

This book is about competitive swimming and its chapters cover the physiological and psychological requirements of the swimmer, the theories of the strokes and training, the talents required by the coach, information to help swimmers' parents and the demands made by various competitions.

The book should be of particular assistance to readers who contemplate taking a swimming coach's qualification, to those recently qualified and perhaps lacking in experience, to swimming clubs and bathside instructors, to schools interested in competitive swimming, to swimmers and their parents and to all other people interested in speed swimming.

As many competitive swimmers now swim an equivalent distance of half the perimeter of the world during their training life, it is hoped that this book will also help to add much more variety to the training schedules of present and future competitive swimmers.

Prologue

As you read this book, you would do well to remember at every page that the following statements are applicable, particularly in competitive swimming:
   (1) Not all swimmers are physically identical.
   (2) Not all swimmers are physiologically identical.
   (3) Not all swimmers are identical as regards mobility.
   (4) Not all swimmers are psychologically identical.
   (5) Not all swimmers have that certain 'feel' for water.
   (6) Not all swimmers have the same degree of competitive spirit.
   (7) Not all swimmers have the same intelligence.
   (8) Not all swimmers have the same dedication to training.
   (9) Stroke technique is necessarily variable within certain limits for each swimmer.
  (10) Not all swimmers have keen, interested parents.
  (11) Some swimmers have *too* keen, anxious parents.

Chapter 1

The Swimming Body: Stamina and Endurance

A most important part of the competitive swimmer's physiological make-up is that marvellous muscle, and the greatest pump ever invented by Nature—the heart.

To succeed in competitive swimming an extra-efficient cardiac system is necessary. Research among past and present world champions shows that all had, to a greater or lesser extent, the same asset of a very efficient heart.

The term 'very efficient heart' means, in fact, that their normal resting pulse was very low and that their recovery from maximum physical effort, where heartbeats of 240 a minute are known in training, was also quite speedy.

A good normal resting pulse for a young intending champion would be around 40 to 50 beats a minute, while a recovery from 230 beats a minute to 120 beats a minute in 45 seconds would be a very sound basis for a promising eleven-year-old champion to work from. (*Note*: 120 beats a minute is a generally accepted level at which to restart training of a fast interval nature, not only in swimming but also in athletics.)

The heart is a muscle and can be improved in its capacity to undertake work as can other muscles. Swimming training itself improves cardiac efficiency, but then again so do circuit exercises, which take less time to do and can be done at home.

Circuit exercises for the heart should be grouped to form a special cardiac circuit. This also means that no exercise which does not specifically keep the heart working should be included in the circuit. Speedier long-term heart improvement will result if such heart exercises are grouped and not interrupted by a 'local muscle' group exercise.

A typical heart circuit for an advanced swimmer would be as follows: Exercise A—15 Skip Jumps, Exercise B—25 Burpees, Exercise C—50 Step-ups, all carried out one after another. The circuit would be repeated a total of, say, three times, starting each circuit on a 120 pulse beat.

Remembering that all swimmers differ, physically and physiologically, the beginner should set up his own circuit in the following way:

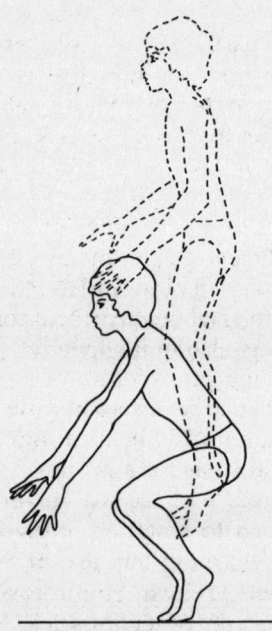

Exercise A: Skip Jumps

(a) Do as many Skip Jumps as you can, *counting them*, until you feel you have lost 'form'. Make a note of your count. ('Form' would be defined as loss of style, rhythm, strength, ability to repeat, etc.)

(b) Wait until you have completely recovered by pulse check and work on Burpees in the same way—count the number you do until form is lost.

The Swimming Body: Stamina and Endurance

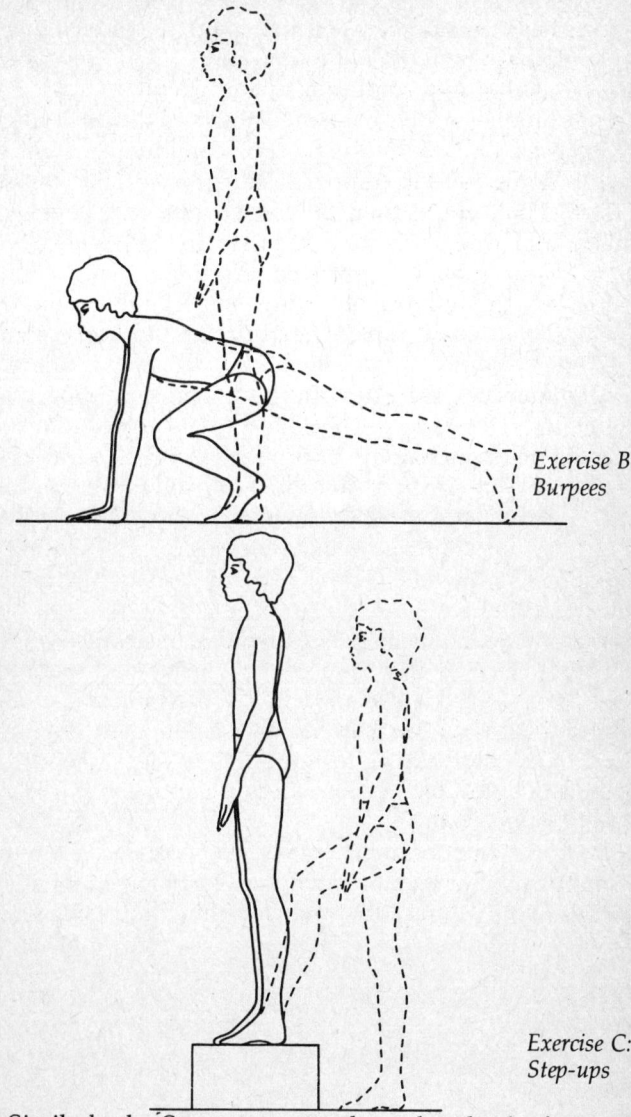

Exercise B: Burpees

Exercise C: Step-ups

(c) Similarly the Step-ups—start by pulse check after resting and count the number you do until form is lost.

(d) Halve the numbers counted in (a), (b) and (c); that is the number you then do by joining the three exercises together in a continuous heart circuit.

For example, suppose when testing you did 20 Skip Jumps, 30 Burpees, and 60 Step-ups. Your continuous circuit would then become 10 Skip Jumps, 15 Burpees and 30 Step-ups.

The circuit could then be carried out once weekly until ability improved, then increased to up to three times a week as progression in ability improved. As stamina and endurance improved, the number of circuits could be increased on any one night to three complete heart circuits starting each one on a 120 pulse count.

All endurance and strength circuits must be progressive to maintain interest, so re-check and re-test every four months and see if you increase your original exercise count, in which case alter your circuit to suit the increased repetition counts.

The advanced competitive swimmer should do circuit work three or four times a week, reducing or eliminating them altogether immediately prior to important competitions (say the preceding week).

Modern research has established that in all athletic sports or pastimes or even the exercise of ordinary day-to-day life, a week of enforced muscle inactivity results in a faster loss of strength and stamina than has ever before been envisaged. It used to be said that we lost strength at the same rate as we gained it, but in fact we lose strength and stamina at a faster rate than we gain it.

Do not, therefore, build up your physiological stamina and strength if you do not intend to carry on your activities, because you will rapidly lose everything you have gained.

Chapter 2

The Swimming Body: Strength

Obviously the swimming body, which has acquired an efficient cardiac system enabling it to cope with the rigours of training and the periodic peak loads of competition, would be of little use and have little success without the strength and muscle power necessary to propel it through the water. Accordingly the competitive swimmer must acquire sufficient muscle strength to achieve his targets.

A muscle is made up of small muscle fibres which contract to work. The fibres can be compared in size to a thick human hair and the strength of the muscle increases as does the diameter of the individual fibres. A muscle fibre will only increase in diameter (and thus strength) as a result of working against a resistance; for example, lifting a weight. The swimming body can increase muscle power in the following ways:

(a) Swimming training—water work (small increase only).
(b) Muscle circuit exercises—using own body weight.
(c) Muscle exercises—using proprietary articles such as weights, pulley weights, Strand exercisers, etc.

Muscle circuit work and the use of muscle strengthening apparatus must be carefully arranged and planned for competitive swimmers, particularly females. Certainly only the *prime mover* muscles of value to a swimmer should be progressively exercised. No value would be obtained from a general body-building programme which would add muscle bulk and weight to those body parts which were of no direct assistance to swimming propulsion.

Additionally, my experience has shown that only those proprietary muscle exercisers should be used which allow the swimmer to simulate actual stroke movements, for example, adaptations to the use of Strand exercisers, pulley weights and Latissimus machines.

Muscles can be increased in strength by correct exercises; therefore the muscle circuits can be built up for each individual in a similar manner to the heart circuits.

Again, no exercise should be included in the circuit which does not directly work a muscle group. Speedier strength increase will be gained by grouped exercises aimed at local muscle groups.

A muscle circuit, using the swimmer's own body weight, can be built up at home from the following exercises, which will increase muscle strength in the main chest, back and arm muscles of value to the swimmer. A typical muscle circuit for an advanced swimmer would be: Exercise A—10 Dips, Exercise B—15 Pulls, Exercise C—25 Press-ups, all carried out one after another. The circuit could be repeated a total of three times, starting each complete circuit on a 120 pulse.

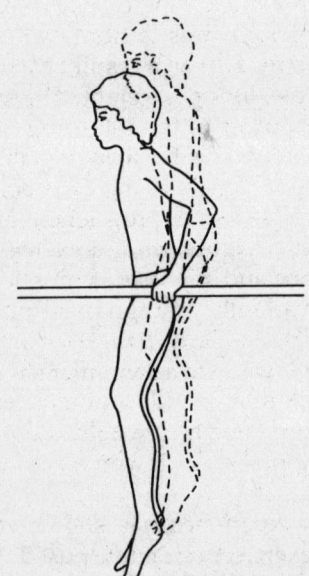

Exercise A: Dips

The Swimming Body: Strength

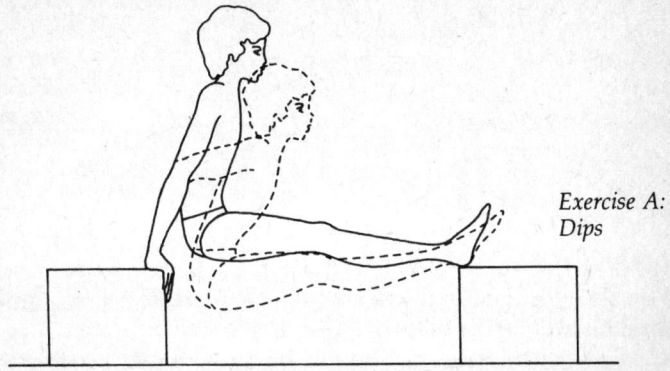

Exercise A: Dips

Exercise A—***Dips***, could be carried out on anything simulating parallel bars, or between two low rigid stools. Lower the suspended body and then raise again, to the floor if on low stools and to the lower chest if on bars.

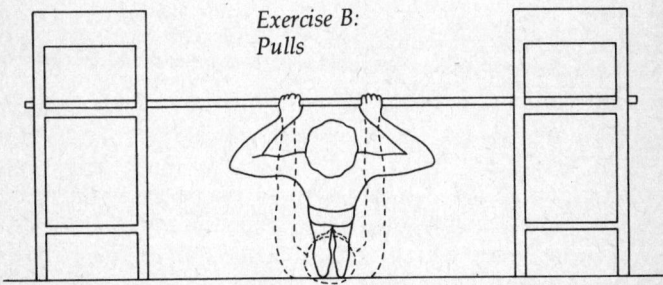

Exercise B: Pulls

Exercise B—***Pulls***, could be carried out by resting a bar across two chairs. Lie supine under the bar. Overgrasp the bar, pull the chest up to the bar and lower again.

Exercise C—***Press-ups***. Lie prone on the floor. Place the hands roughly under the shoulders. Press the chest and body away from the floor and then lower again. The body must not be allowed to flex. Try to make the chest leave the floor last on pressing up, and be the first to touch it on lowering.

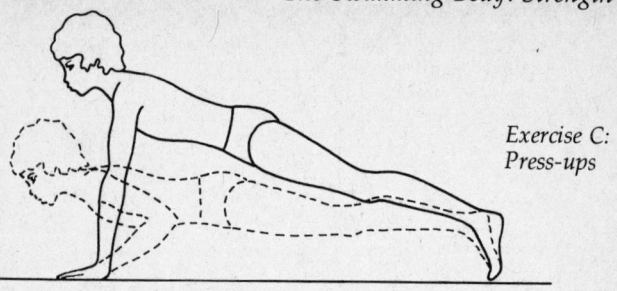

Exercise C: Press-ups

The beginner should build up his muscle circuit as previously described in the heart circuit exercises, testing himself on each exercise until form is lost, halving the number done on each exercise, then combining all three exercises into one circuit. He should carry out the circuit once weekly until strength begins to improve, then increase the number to one circuit three times a week. As strength is gained, increase the number of circuits a night until three complete muscle circuits are done, three nights a week. Carry out the heart circuits and the muscle circuits one after the other.

Weight-lifting exercises of value to the competitive swimmer are:

(1) *Two-hand Press*—When in a standing position, press the bar and weights above the head from a support position across the chest. (General arm and chest muscles.)

(2) *Two-hand Curl*—Undergrasp the bar and weights. From a standing position with the bar in a free hanging position, raise the weight to the chest using the elbows as a pivot point. (Arm muscles.)

(3) *Two-hand Transverse Fix*—Overgrasp the bar and weights. From a standing position, with the bar in a free hanging position, move the weight through 90 degrees using the elbows as a pivot point. (Arm muscles.)

(4) *Straddle Lift*—From a straddle position astride the bar and weights, squat down and grasp the bar, lift the bar and weights by straightening the legs, keeping the back straight. (Leg muscles—major benefit to Breaststrokers.)

The Swimming Body: Strength

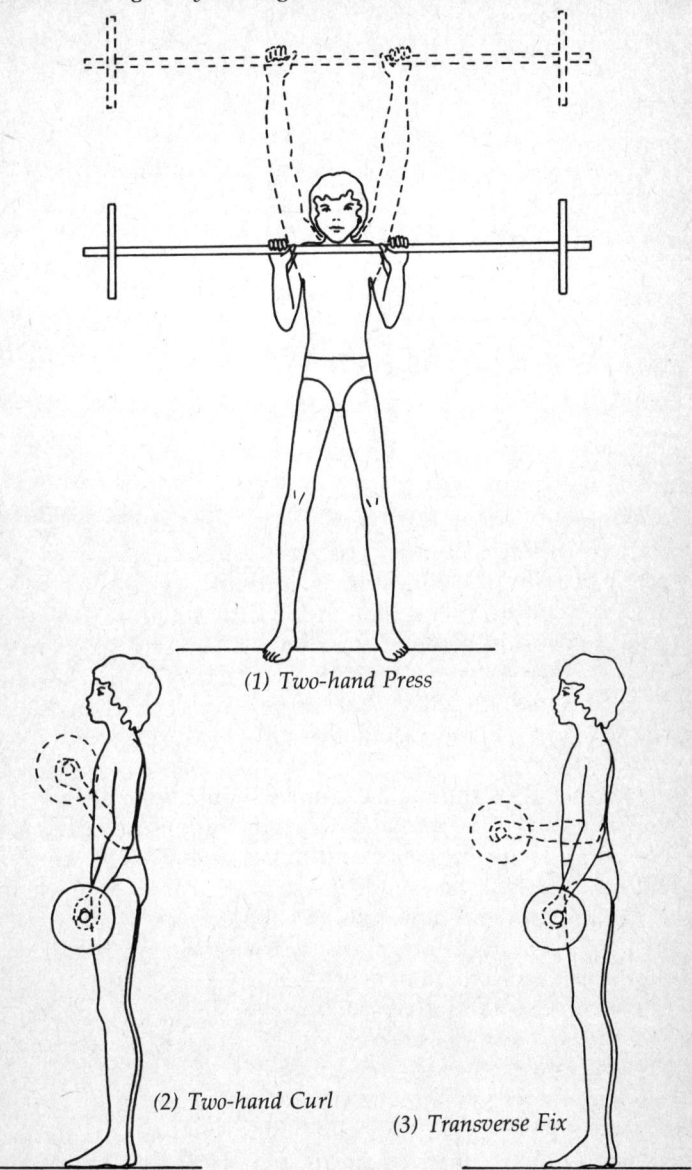

(1) Two-hand Press

(2) Two-hand Curl

(3) Transverse Fix

The Swimming Body: Strength

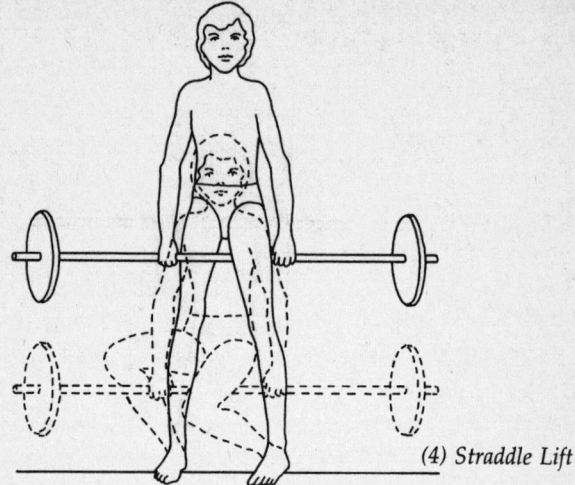

(4) Straddle Lift

Any intending swimming coach would be well advised to work with a physical education weight-lifting specialist before trying to teach his own swimmers. There is a great deal to be learned, covering correct lifting techniques and safety with weights. Always have assistants (or catchers) when dealing with beginners, to catch the bar-bells in case of accident. Always begin with an extremely light weight to master technique first.

In the exercises shown, a beginner should find the heaviest weight he can lift for a total of three repetitions on each exercise, *testing* as for the heart and muscle exercises. When the weight is decided, he should take two-thirds of that weight and do a set of repetitions totalling about seven on each exercise. By re-testing as strength improves, he can build up a weight-training schedule.

To gain strength in a muscle, as opposed to body-building, go for the heaviest weight over a few repetitions, as opposed to a light weight over many repetitions.

My experience has shown that a most satisfactory method of using weights in connection with building muscle strength for swimmers is to construct one's own Latissimus machine,

The Swimming Body: Strength

which uses weights on steel wire so that a stroke movement can be copied.

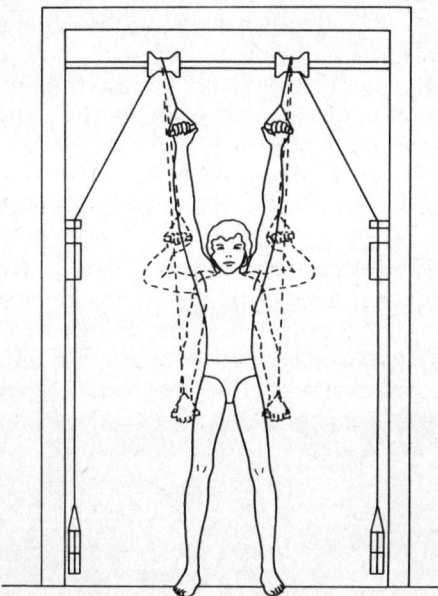

Latissimus Machine

A double arm pull-push would be used to simulate Butterfly Stroke and, by using the weights alternately, single arm Backstroke can be copied.

The learner should, as in previous exercises, start off with a very light weight to master technique. A test should then be made to find the heaviest weight to be moved over three repetitions.

When this weight is ascertained, take two-thirds of the weight and use it over a total of seven repetitions on each exercise. When once it is set up, this form of apparatus can be used quite quickly, and the swimmer can do so about four times weekly. As strength increases, re-test every three to four months so that the weight lifted is progressively increased. This machine is absolutely useless for this purpose unless the swimmer performs the pull-push action correctly. The hand must move in front of the elbow joint and lead the way in the movement.

To counteract boredom, because circuit exercises can become very boring over a period, alter the circuits, working on the principle of a reducing set series.

For example, the typical heart circuit for an advanced swimmer shown earlier can occasionally be carried out as follows to relieve monotony:

Exercise A—15 Skip Jumps becomes 20, then 15, then 10 Skip Jumps with a rest interval of 20 seconds between each.

Exercise B—25 Burpees becomes 30, then 25, then 20 Burpees with a rest interval of 20 seconds between each.

Exercise C—50 Step-ups becomes 55, then 50, then 45 Step-ups with a rest interval of 20 seconds between each.

This forms an alternative to the three complete circuits of the exercises detailed on page 12.

Chapter 3

The Swimming Body: Breathing and Variational Activities

All the previous exercises for the heart and local muscles carried out in a circuit lose a lot of their value to the competitive swimmer if not closely related to regular breathing patterns. The swimmer breathes to a pattern in the water and should do the same sort of thing when exercising. Regular breathing when exercising will encourage rib-cage development and lung capacity when young. Large lung capacity is of obvious use to the swimmer; the larger the air intake, the greater the proportion of oxygen in the body, which means an adequate supply of oxygen at the muscle capillaries for the formation of energy. This is of greater value to the distance swimmer than to the sprinter.

My experience has shown that swimmers when exercising are notoriously lazy breathers and must be encouraged to breathe more deeply when carrying out circuit work.

There are additional ways of encouraging stamina, endurance and breathing for swimmers which have become known as variational activities. Running and basketball I have found to be the most useful and enjoyable and they can be fitted quite easily into a land conditioning session involving circuits and mobility.

Running can be general distance work, accompanied by *regular* breathing in time to a number of strides, and can be varied by introducing sprints for short distances followed by easier slow runs, in other words introduce 'fartlek' (fast/slow repeats) into your running.

Another variation in running to keep the interest is to introduce 'pacing' to the swimmer. Run a mile on the watch, timed, then break the distance down into 8 × 220 yards, with 20-second rest intervals as a repeat exercise. The idea is to ensure that none of the 220s is slower than the mile time divided by 8. We use the above practice regularly in swimming training and it can be generally used in land conditioning sessions.

Basketball sessions in land conditioning work-outs will be both popular and valuable: popular from the 'variation from monotony' point of view, and valuable from the point of view of speeding up the swimmers' movements and reactions.

Chapter 4

The Swimming Body: Mobility

Mobility, or flexibility, is of extreme importance to the competitive swimmer and could be said to be a very close third in importance after strength and stamina. Flexibility or mobility exercises should be performed every day by the swimmer, particularly before doing circuit work, or weight work, and also before swimming. The value of doing mobility exercises before going to a swim competition cannot be too highly stressed.

Briefly, and here again comprehensive books can be read on this, to improve mobility in any movement of a limb, the 'antagonist' muscle group must be stretched. The muscles of our body involved in limb movements can be said to be arranged in 'opposing' groups. Where a group work to perform a certain limb movement, the 'opposing' group (those which would work to reverse the same limb movement) should be relaxed.

These opposite muscle groups are the ones which must be stretched to improve mobility in any certain limb movement. All mobility exercises, or stretching exercises, should therefore be performed *SLOWLY* because opposite muscle groups tend to contract impulsively in order to safeguard limb movements where fast limb actions are carried out.

My experience has shown that when carrying out any specific movement, mobility (or stretching) exercises give better results by isolating the body and limbs not concerned in the movement. The following mobility exercises should be of great value to all swimmers.

FIG. 1—*Neck, Spinal Vertebrae, Hamstrings* Sit on the floor, with the legs straight and knees pressed to the floor,

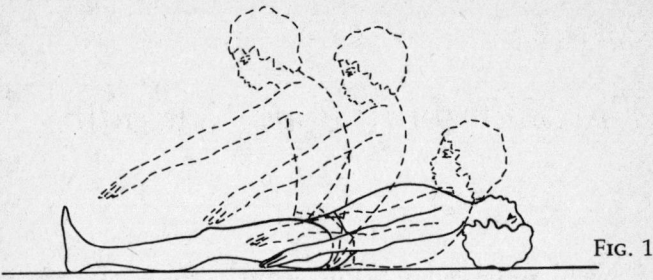

FIG. 1

reach forward and test your forward reach to your toes. Then lie flat on your back, arms at your sides. Alternately, arch your head backwards, raising your chest and arching your spine off of the floor, then lift the head and shoulders to look at your feet with the spine flat on the floor. Increase the range of movement each time until a sitting upright position is reached. As a last stretching movement in this position, open the legs wide, exhale, and try to collapse the chest and upper trunk to the floor between your legs, finally assuming a 'crab' position. Lastly stand upright with your legs fairly wide apart. Lower your trunk and arms forward until your hands touch the floor, reaching out as far as you can. Holding this position, continue to touch the floor and progress your hands towards your feet until you are touching the floor under your body and behind a point in line with your feet. Re-assume your original sitting position and re-test your forward reach to your toes. Considerable improvement can be made when originally commencing this exercise.

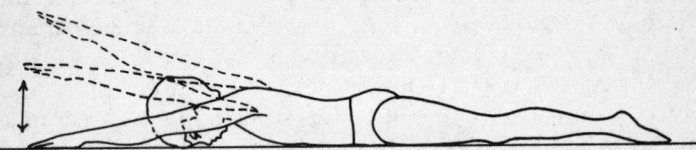

FIG. 2—***Shoulder Extension*** Lie prone on the floor, arms extended above the head with the forehead pressed to the floor. Raise the hands and the arms off the floor as high as possible. Holding this position, press the hands and arms

The Swimming Body: Mobility

upwards as high as possible trying to gain further extension, then relax. Repeat as necessary.

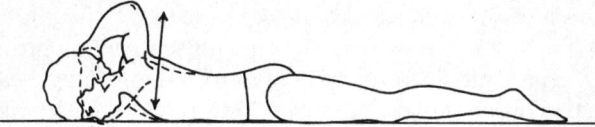

FIG. 3—*Shoulder Mobility*   Lie prone on the floor, the hands resting behind the head, fingertips touching, the elbows relaxed and resting on the floor. Raise the elbows as high as possible. Holding this position, press upwards with the elbows trying to gain increased movement. Relax to the floor and repeat as necessary.

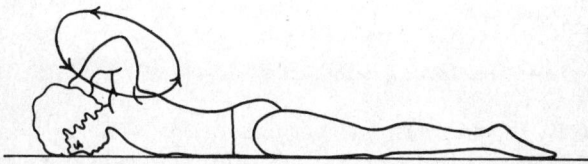

FIG. 4—*Shoulder Mobility*   Lie prone on the floor, forehead pressed to the floor. Place the hands behind the head, fingertips touching. Raise the elbows off the floor and move the elbows in a circular path drawing as big a circle as possible. The movement, if performed properly, will cause the scapula to move freely forward and backward. Relax the elbows to the floor and, after a short rest, repeat the above but drawing imaginary circles with the elbows in an opposite direction to those previously. Do at least 20 circular movements on each.

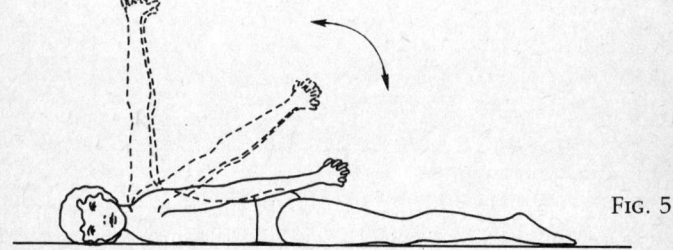

FIG. 5

FIG. 5—**Shoulder Mobility**   Lie prone on the floor, with the head resting sideways on the floor. The arms, fingers interlocked, lie across the back of the lumbar vertebrae. Raise the arms to a position as high as possible above the head. Try to reach the vertical position. Holding this position, press the hands and arms even further forward, trying to go past the vertical position. Relax and repeat the stretching movement as required.

FIG. 6—**Hip Joint Mobility, Knee Flexion**   Lie prone on the floor, legs straight together, but with the arms stretched out sideways, palms down, pressed to the floor. Raise the right leg, bending the knee and try to place the foot on the back of the head. The head and chest arch backward to assist this. When this movement is completed to its full range, cross the right leg across the body until the right toe touches the left hand. Return the leg to its original position. Repeat the above with the left leg and then repeat both legs as required.

FIG. 7—**Neck Mobility**   Lie prone on the floor. With the hands palm down on the floor and close to the hips, press the

upper trunk upwards vertically away from the floor by straightening the arms. The pelvis must remain as close to the floor as possible. Turn the head sideways, looking right and left alternately, trying to increase the movement range all the time. The chin must go past the shoulder for good movement.

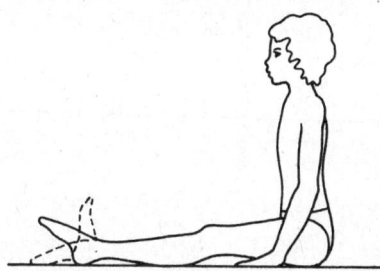

FIG. 8—*Ankle Mobility* Sit on the floor, legs extended straight in front. Balance with arms to the floor at the sides. Alternately plantar-flex and dorsi-flex the feet. Full range of movement is required. Dorsi-flexion is required for Breaststrokers but plantar-flexion is required for the other strokes. Change position and kneel down with bent knees, on the heels, keeping the insteps pressed flat to the floor with the buttocks. Change position again, sitting cross-legged on the floor. Rotate one ankle by moving the foot in a circular manner with the hands, then, holding the lower leg, shake the ankle 'loose'. Repeat with the other leg.

FIG. 9—*Neck Mobility* Stand upright in a relaxed manner. Arch the head backwards trying to touch the back of the head to the cervical vertebrae. Drop the head forward touching the chin to the breast bone. Repeat the movement at least 20 times.

FIG. 10—*Neck Mobility* Stand upright in a relaxed manner. Roll the head around the shoulders in a circular path, trying to put the chin to the chest, the right ear to the right shoulder, the back of the head to the cervical vertebrae, and the left ear to the left shoulder, in consecutively smooth actions. Relax and rest and repeat in the opposite direction. Carry out at least 10 times.

Fig. 11—*Shoulder Mobility* Stand upright. Circle the arms, using the shoulder as the centre of the circle, moving

The Swimming Body: Mobility

one arm clockwise, the other anti-clockwise. The movement is easiest started off for beginners by raising both the arms above the head, then moving one arm forward and downward and the other backward and downward and continuing. At least 20 or 30 revolutions are required.

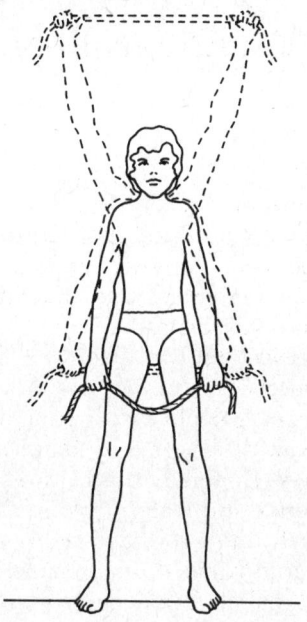

FIG. 12—*Shoulder Mobility* Stand upright. A length of rope must be held between the hands across the front of the thighs. Raise both arms simultaneously upwards and backwards, without losing grasp of the rope, until the rope is moved backwards over the head with the arms hanging loosely down, and the rope across the back of the thighs. One or two trial movements should be made to determine a comfortable length of rope to leave between the hands. When this is determined, carry out at least 30 to 40 movements in a reasonably fast manner. The correct amount of rope is that which is neither too loose nor too easy, nor that which is too short, causing too much discomfort.

Chapter 5

The Swimming Body: Power/Weight Ratio

In competitive swimming, where the body is carrying out movements in order to produce speed through the water, there is a balance between body weight and power available with buoyancy and body shape also affecting performance, although to a much lesser degree.

Only two factors assist buoyancy in the water as far as the human frame is concerned and they are air contained in the lungs and fat. Eleven-year-old girls frequently record faster times over identical distances on identical strokes than eleven-year-old boys. Generally this can easily be seen to be due to better buoyancy and watermanship on the part of the girls. The girl is usually more rounded at this age than the boy. When the boy grows and develops more muscle strength so he by-passes the girl in performance by virtue of superior strength, although his buoyancy and watermanship may still be inferior.

Obviously as children grow, the body weight increases and power or strength should also increase for swimming performance to be maintained. Unfortunately we often have cases of children where extremely rapid growth takes place with corresponding body weight increase, but the muscles and strength do not improve at the same rate. In other words the child 'outgrows strength'. This can be a very trying time for the young competitor and performance will stand still, or even worsen, until the power/weight ratio is restored.

It is a fact that many swimming parents cannot accept that these physical and physiological changes can upset swimming

The Swimming Body: Power/Weight Ratio

development and many swimmers have been lost to the sport by impatient, ill-advised parents.

Alteration in body weight, shape, physiological change and buoyancy can and do alter the performance of swimmers. What may be a number one stroke one year for the younger competitor may, by virtue of physical and physiological change, become the number two or number three stroke the next year, all of which must be accepted by parents and watched carefully by coaches.

All young swimmers should therefore train and compete on all strokes. For senior swimmers, where growth is completed or practically completed, then weight is of the utmost importance. Weight should be checked every week and any difference must be accounted for. Girls are much more liable to weight change than boys in this respect.

There are exceptions to every rule and these seem to occur more frequently in swimming than other sports, but generally speaking the taller, heavier, muscular type of swimmer will do well over the short distance—100 metres, 200 metres—whereas the smaller competitor, or taller swimmer with less muscle development, will do better over the long distances—400 metres, 800 metres, 1,500 metres. This is only applicable in terms of body weight and shape; when individual temperament or psychology enters into the matter then different results may occur.

Particularly in boys, the popular athletic-type figure with massive broad shoulders tapering down to narrow hips may not in fact become the national swimming champion. Statistics have shown that a predominance of men champions have in fact been the narrow-shouldered and wider-hipped type.

Chapter 6

The Swimming Body: Diet

Throughout my long experience of competitive swimming, I have frequently read or have been told that providing a competitive swimmer had a good, well-balanced diet there should be no need for any added specialities; my swimmers have always been so advised, and yet on my own squad I have numerous swimmers who have been found to lack essential vitamins.

The two most common vitamins which I would recommend the competitive swimmer to take are:

Vitamin C Daily supplements are required to help resistance to colds.

Iron Anaemia, or an anaemic condition, is shortage of red blood corpuscles in the blood stream. To the competitive swimmer, lack of red corpuscles is lack of oxygen-carrying capacity to the muscles and therefore loss of energy. I have had instances of my squad swimmers, both girls and boys, who were found to have an anaemic condition. Daily multi-vitamin tablets containing a percentage of iron can guard against this.

It is now believed that energy is supplied in the main from glycogen body reserves when exercising. Glycogen body reserves are produced and stored mainly from the consumption of the carbohydrate foods—sugar, bread, cereals, potatoes, cakes, etc.—which readily convert to glycogen in the human body.

However, we can see the danger, to girls especially, of the above foods, which can quite quickly affect body weight, so care must be taken with certain body types of the amounts which are eaten.

Proprietary liquids and tablets are marketed which are easily

The Swimming Body: Diet

digestible sources of energy and I believe that there is a useful form of food here for the competitive swimmer. Not only can such liquids be used on competitive days—between morning, afternoon and evening sessions—they can also be used prior to early morning training, for example, to give the swimmer that little something in the stomach before training starts. All such foods need time to be converted in the body to glycogen, so they should be introduced into the diet, if so desired, well before the competition occurs.

The actual value of such foods as energy givers is open to some degree of question, but on the issue of their being easily digested food, prior to exercise, there can be no doubt. There is of course the psychological aspect. If the competitor believes that his performance will go well as a result of taking such foods, then it would surely be foolish to try to convert him from them.

The competitive swimmer should have a well-balanced diet to maintain health and energy; fads and fancies in food must not be considered and concentrating on certain foods for calorific value gains must also not be considered, because such actions can produce an unbalanced diet. No competitive swimmer in training for serious competition should go on a weight-reducing diet; such an undertaking must be done gradually and at the correct time relating to competition. Meals should be eaten at least three hours before competition for an adequate margin of digestion and should preferably contain a high percentage of carbohydrates.

A diet containing all the essentials to health for the competitive swimmer should be made up from the following:

Proteins (Body builders for wear and tear)   Chemical compounds comprising nitrogen, carbon, hydrogen and oxygen. *Examples:* meat, fish, cheese, peas, beans and to a lesser degree bread, butter, eggs and milk.

Carbohydrates (Energy givers)   Carbon, hydrogen and oxygen. *Examples:* sugar, bread, cereals and potatoes.

Fats (For heat and energy)   Chiefly derived from animal sources. *Examples:* animal fat, butter, cheese and eggs —these act as energy reserves for health and growth.

Water   Contained in most proteins and carbohydrates.

Vitamins are complex substances essential for life, health and growth but are not in themselves sources of energy.

Vitamin A   General health promoter and any normal diet should contain adequate quantities. Serious lack of Vitamin A can produce poor resistance to infection. *Examples:* animal fats, milk, cream, butter, eggs, liver, spinach, cod-liver oil.

Vitamin B   Adequate amounts found in wheat, yeast, peanuts, rice, eggs. Serious lack of Vitamin B can produce nervous disorders and skin troubles.

Vitamin C   Adequate amounts found in fresh fruit and vegetables, particularly oranges, lemons, blackcurrants, apples, tomatoes, cabbage and lettuce. Serious lack of Vitamin C can weaken resistance to infection from colds, virus infections, etc.

Vitamin D   Found in fish-liver oil and eggs. Essential for bone growth and development. Serious lack of Vitamin D could result in bones becoming soft.

Minerals   Common salt, calcium, phosphorus, iron and iodine. Calcium and phosphorus are found in milk, iron in meat, vegetables and fruits, and iodine in municipal drinking water.

Chapter 7

The Swimming Body: Psychological

To succeed in competitive sport the essential requirement is competitive spirit.

As far as is known, all people have competitive spirit but in varying degrees. The measure of success in sport is determined by the degree of this spirit in the competitor.

In competitive swimming, apart from team races, all events are individual, so that not only does the swimmer have to have competitive spirit, he also needs the temperament to stand in front of spectators and fellow competitors as an individual and show what he can do.

Not only does the swimmer require that competitive urge, he also requires temperament, plus the ability to concentrate on his own performance and not freeze with nerves, or worry about other competitors.

Generally speaking, assuming one is a good competitor, then well-chosen competition at gradually increasing higher levels should produce more experienced, mature and confident competitors. In fact, any competitive swimmer's programme should be planned. Starting, for example, with local club galas a swimmer should proceed to County Age Groups, District Age Groups, National Age Groups, National Championships, and International Meets, along his career.

My experience has shown that there are dangers in too much competition generally and in particular in too much competition at the same level. A swimmer, instead of developing to successive higher levels of competition, can become so accustomed to competition of a similar nature or level that the competitive edge is dulled and the swimmer becomes blasé and indifferent about whether success is obtained or not.

For example, if your club only competes in, say, swimming leagues, then ultimately your swimmers will become swimming-league minded, accustomed only to certain distance competition, and this is a disservice to your swimmers and to swimming in general.

The swimmer with the correct competitive approach or temperament expects to be nervous and to have a few 'butterflies', but when he approaches the start block he should be able to concentrate on the way he will swim his race and the few final things his coach has told him.

The competitor who approaches the block with no race plan in his mind, watching everyone around him and worrying about them, will not win because this competitor has not yet learnt to master himself, never mind his fellow competitors.

So the mind of the successful competitor must be hardened, confident and capable of concentration, built up from the past experience of a well-planned competitive programme.

My squad are advised at the outset of their swimming careers to set themselves a target—a number of successive targets if necessary—with a final goal. Then their careers and training must persevere towards this goal and defeats or successes on the way must be taken in their stride.

This plan is a successful way to build up the correct competitive approach in young swimmers. The only stumbling blocks which my experience has encountered have been the parents of swimmers. When will parents learn that there is no disgrace in a young swimmer's mind when he is beaten by a fellow competitor? The disgrace is all in the parents' minds and it is almost as if they are the ones competing.

All great champions have been beaten on occasions in their careers, or done disappointing times, or misplanned a race, and have come back all the harder for it.

Chapter 8

The Swimming Body: The Swimming Strokes

The swimming strokes will not be discussed in great detail because many comprehensive volumes have already done just this, but I will make certain comments on all the strokes, particularly in those cases where my experience has shown that all that one reads may not prove to be so in practice.

Additionally, as this book is intended to give assistance to intending coaches, the strokes will be discussed under the following main headings:
(1) Poise (Body position)
(2) Leg Action
(3) Arm Action
(4) Breathing
(5) Timing

and in that particular order, because it is the order of assessing a stroke which you will be required to use when taking your Club Coaches' or ASA Coaches' examination.

As a coach you will be required, both in examination or in later bathside practice, to write down or memorize all the above points in a swimmer's stroke after watching him swim for six to eight lengths of a pool.

It is much better to have a prepared plan of what to look for under these main headings by writing down a number of subheadings, which you must look for and cover in the allowable time. We are talking of *stroke analysis*, and before taking examinations obtain as much practical experience in this as you can.

The table which follows shows a tabulated list of stroke

analysis points which you must cover on any of the four competitive swimming strokes.

(1) Poise (Body position)
  (a) Describe the body position relative to the water surface.
  (b) Describe the head position.
  (c) Legs too low or too high.
  (d) Hips too low or too high.
  (e) Body roll (applicable to Front Crawl and Backstroke). Comment on degree of roll.

(2) Leg Action
  (a) Legality: is it legal, symmetrical (Butterfly and Breast Stroke)?
  (b) Depth of kick.
  (c) Amount of knee bend.
  (d) Proportion of movement from hip or knee (Butterfly, Backstroke and Front Crawl).
  (e) Ankles—flexibility.
  (f) Number of leg kicks per arm cycle (Butterfly, Backstroke and Front Crawl).
  (g) Type of leg kick (Breast Stroke): 'whip' kick or otherwise.

(3) Arm Action
  (a) Entry point (Butterfly, Backstroke, Front Crawl).
  (b) Exit point (Butterfly, Backstroke, Front Crawl).
  (c) Type of pull/push phase (Butterfly—'keyhole' pattern; Backstroke—bent arm, 'S' type; Front Crawl—inverted question mark' type).
  (d) Catch-point: where does catch-point occur?
  (e) Hand position: does angle of hand alter through the pull/push?
  (f) Recovery (Front Crawl—high elbow, Backstroke—straight arm).
  (g) Legality, symmetry (Butterfly, Breast Stroke).

The Swimming Body: The Swimming Strokes

(4) Breathing
  (a) When does the breath occur in the stroke cycle, at what phase of the stroke?
  (b) What breathing pattern is being used (Front Crawl—'bilateral' etc, Butterfly—'alternate')?
  (c) Type of breathing—controlled exhalation, 'explosive'.
  (d) Position of mouth relative to water surface when breathing.

(5) Timing
  (a) Amount of catch-up in Front Crawl.
  (b) How do they time in Backstroke? Is one hand entering the water as the other leaves at the thigh?
  (c) Breast Stroke—where does leg kick terminate relative to the arm action?
  (d) Butterfly—number and type of leg kick per arm cycle.

BUTTERFLY

Poise (Body position) Modern literature seems to recommend a flatter type of body position with little undulation. My experience in this stroke suggests that the swimmer will form his own body movement depending on body type. The taller, more flexible body type is liable to undulate more than the shorter, stockier type. As long as performance is good, I do not question undulation. If the chest is being exposed on taking a breath that is a different matter. I prefer to see the chin in the water when breathing.

A pair of hips which stays low in the water needs modification as this position could give rise to considerable 'drag' from water eddies formed. My preference is for some undulation from the hips, a definite rise and fall.

Similarly, a pair of legs which kicks down, and stays down until the next kick, also needs alteration. If there has to be a semi-glide in the leg kick, then let it be when the feet are high and not low. A pair of legs and feet staying low cause more 'drag'.

Head position should align itself because the thinking swimmer will have his eyes looking ahead for catch-point by the hands anyway.

Leg Action   Emphasis of power on the down kick with good ankle flexibility. A genuine two-beat leg kick, or a one-beat plus a semi, is looked for by most coaches, especially over the 200-metre distance. The first 50 metres of both 200-metre and 100-metre distances are performed by some swimmers with a single kick because they can obtain faster arm repetitions by so doing.

An important point in the leg action is not to let the legs trail in the down position after a kick. This can lead to drag from eddying water at the back of the legs and thighs. My squad are coached to recover their legs to normal position as soon as the down kick is completed; if there has to be a glide or pause in the leg kick, it is better at high level than low level. We also coach a leg kick which has a little more knee bend over the 100-metres swims, than over the 200-metres distance, where more action from the hip is stressed. To comply with ASA laws, symmetry is required in the leg action.

Arm Action   Symmetrical action from both arms is required to comply with ASA laws. Butterfly simultaneous arm action, as opposed to alternate action of Backstroke, requires a fast recovery of the arms and a strong repetitive stroke. Any loss of momentum in a swim is extremely difficult to regain. Hand entry is required between the body centre-line and the shoulder. Young children invariably go in wide until more mature strength develops. Hand exit should be at the thigh, at the end of the 'push' phase, and my squad are all coached to brush their thighs with the thumb on exit. In all swimming strokes it is important that the hand takes command of the arm actions at catch-point. Catch-point is on, or just below, the surface in Butterfly and the hands must feel for this, palm down. The hands change position through the arm pull/push, the swimmer endeavouring to preserve the palm of the hand pulling or pushing towards his own feet. Hand movement is all connected through the swimmer's brain and his feel for the water.

Also, for forward movement in swimming, force must be directed in the opposite direction. (Newton's Laws of Motion—action and reaction are equal and opposite.)

The most important points in the arm action are—does the hand take command at catch-point and do the hand and forearm lead the way in the pull/push as opposed to the elbow joint leading?

The path of the hand through the water after entry varies with many swimmers. The pattern generally established is that initially the hands move wider apart but, as they begin to lead the way in the pull under the chest, the hands converge until the fingertips may be almost touching under the stomach, then widening to brush the thighs on exit. The path of the pull has been described as the 'keyhole'-type pull when viewed from above the swimmer.

Breathing The breath is taken at the end of the arm pull/push when the hands are at the thigh.

Breath is taken jointly by head up and down movement and body undulation. Try to keep the chin in the water even when breathing.

Watch out for 'too-early' breathing which can lead to an interrupted, ineffective arm pull/push.

A breath can be taken at every stroke, or taken alternately at the start of a race over the first 50 metres.

If you decide not to breath at every stroke, then I believe you must decide on a definite plan or breathing pattern and adhere to it.

Timing A double leg-kick fitted into a continuous arm cycle is the ideal.

One kick occurs at hand entry and one at hand exit. In fact, most Butterfly swimmers have a kick and a semi-kick as opposed to a genuine two-beat kick.

Some swimmers will kick once per arm cycle at the start of a

Butterfly race over the first, say, 50 metres because they can obtain faster repetitive arm action in this way, and then revert to a usual two-beat kick for the rest of the race.

BACKSTROKE

Poise (Body position)   Good poise with a horizontal body position is required here, as most coaches agree. Shoulders should be on the water surface, hips slightly lower below the water surface, the legs tapering downward when kicking to about 18 inches below the surface. The head position is critical and could be variable for each particular body type. Generally speaking, the ears would be on the water surface. Some swimmers find it advantageous to have a slightly raised head position over 100-metre distances, allowing the head to lie farther back over 200-metre distances. A body type with good flotation and buoyancy almost certainly requires a more raised head position than the opposite body type, who should position the head farther back to improve poise.

Most practising coaches advocate a bent arm pull/push (a flattened 'S' path of the hand when viewed from the side) and to this end the body should not stay absolutely flat (supine), but should roll when pulling, around 40 degrees, to deepen the hand below the water surface.

Although the body may roll, the head must not.

Leg Action   Six leg kicks are required in each arm cycle and generally this is what is found, particularly in girls. Emphasis is on the up kick for power. The depth of kick below the water should be about 18 inches. A lot of home-produced swimmers miss out here, I feel, because they all seem to make their kicks too shallow. The value of bending the knee slightly on the down kick, to obtain that more powerful up kick, does not seem to be considered enough. Good ankle flexibility is most important. Work mainly from the hip joint, with a little extra knee bend on the down kick for a good leg action.

The Swimming Body: The Swimming Strokes

Arm Action Arm action in Backstroke is alternate. The hand enters the water in line with the shoulder and leaves at the thigh. Recovery should be fast and relaxed. Catch-point is just below the water surface and every effort must be made to feel for a strong catch-position. The hand must alter position as it travels through the pull/push phase to keep the palm of the hand facing towards the swimmer's own feet, for the reasons outlined under Butterfly. It is generally accepted that a bent arm pull/push is superior to a straight arm. Viewed from the side, the swimmer's hand moves in flattened horizontal 'S' type of movement. ...⁓... Swimmers using this type of pull roll their body when pulling, up to 40 degrees, to deepen the pulling hand below the water surface. This also has the effect of raising the opposite shoulder above the water surface permitting cleaner recovery of the opposite arm. (The head does not roll.)

The arm recovery in Backstroke is generally accepted as palm facing outward, little finger first, but with the stiffer-shoulder body types I have found the swimmer concerned will have a faster, more relaxed recovery by adopting a palm-inward position with the thumb leading the way. Of course the hand must turn smartly on entry to little finger first, palm outward, to effect a good catch-point.

Breathing Absolutely no problem exists in Backstroke because the mouth is above the water all the time. It is surprising how many Backstrokers, young and old, have no regular fixed breathing pattern. However, I coach Backstrokers to adopt a regular breathing pattern from the outset, for example, to breath in and out at every successive right-arm recovery.

Timing Correct timing is vital in Backstroke. Alternate action is the aim, one arm entering above the head as the opposite arm leaves the water at the thigh. Most Backstrokers check timing by feel, as one hand enters the water the other brushes the thigh on exit.

BREAST STROKE

Poise (Body position) It is generally agreed that all body positions should be as horizontal as possible but, unfortunately for speed, this stroke contains leg and arm movements which deviate the body from the ideal position more than in any other stroke. Shoulders should be on the water surface. Hips are below the water surface—a little deeper than Butterfly or Backstroke for the same swimmer. Head should be normal, looking ahead. Ideally, the head moves only to raise the mouth above the water surface for in-breath, then the head relaxes again until the eyes are roughly on the water surface.

Leg Action Must be symmetrical from ASA laws point of view, and FINA law now expects the toes to be turned out sideways during the kick. A complex number of leg muscles are used in this kick.

One very important point is the method of recovering the feet to the gluteus maximus (the principal muscle of the buttocks). This must be accomplished by knee bend, as opposed to drawing the thighs up under the pelvis. The front of the thighs should stay at roughly 40 degrees to the line of the body in the water at maximum leg recovery, otherwise, if the angle is increased by drawing the knees and thighs up further, a large amount of drag and resistance will be caused by the front of the thighs.

Good dorsi and plantar foot-flexion is essential in Breast Stroke—particularly dorsi (the ability to hinge the toes and ankle joint up towards the knee-cap).

In the 'whip'-type leg kick, the knees of the swimmer at the commencement of the kick should be narrower than the feet when viewed from the rear. The feel of the leg kick by the feet is backward, sideways, round and downward in that order. The maximum force is applied towards the end of the kick. The leg kick provides the major propulsion in Breast Stroke.

Arm Action Must be symmetrical to conform to ASA laws.

My squad is coached to concentrate right at the beginning of the pull on moving the *hand first*, in a movement which presses downward and sideways, and backward, with a straight arm, terminating with a bent arm at the end of the arm pull. From this position, the hands move inward until they are below the neck, with the elbows following suit to 'tuck in' to the sides of the body. As the hands push forward in recovery they should be palm down and go slightly deeper. The hands, as in all the other strokes, should move to keep the palm towards the feet in the pull to retain the required feel or water pressure on them. A common fault in Breast Stroke is to bend the arms from the commencement of the arm pull.

Breathing The timing of the breath is important and should be taken at the end of the arm pull. My squad is also coached to breathe at every stroke and never to attempt alternate breaths.

Breathing is co-ordinated with the up and down movement of the head and there should be no additional body movement to assist this. The mouth should rise just above the water surface for in-breath, then disappear below surface again as the swimmer's head moves down to approximately eye on, or just below, the water surface. My squad is coached to take a fast breath on Breast Stroke as opposed to a long leisurely breath, which will keep the rhythm of the stroke more continuous.

Another point to watch on breathing is that the head continues to move forward when breath is taken and does not jerk backward. (Check from the side by watching the head relative to the bathside tiles, etc.)

Timing As vital to Breast Stroke as it is to Backstroke. My squad is simply coached to 'kick the recovering hands forward'. A glide in Breast Stroke is a very important part of checking timing. How much glide the swimmer retains in competition is, I feel, an individual choice. Most coaches would retain a slight glide over the 200-metre distance but minimize it over 100 metres.

The ability to glide in Breast Stroke is dependent on each individual swimmer, relating to buoyancy and power of leg kick. The swimmer with a weaker leg kick has to kick more continuously for good forward propulsion. The individual swimmer has to pull/kick in such a manner of timing which gives good forward momentum and retains the head in an approximately level manner without contravening ASA law.

FRONT CRAWL

Poise (Body position) As horizontal a body position to the water surface as possible is required. The leg and arm movements encourage such a body position in this stroke. Over short distances, shoulders and hips will ride the water surface, but sink only slightly over the 400-metre and 800-metre distances.

Head position is vital and crucial in this stroke. The head should use the water as a pillow—the forehead resting on it. The head must not move up and down throughout the swim but must be steady. Nor must the head move off the centre-line of the spine and body when viewed from above, throughout the swim.

Mention should be made here when talking of head position in relation to body poise that the head does not turn alone when breathing in Front Crawl; the slight turn is assisted by body roll. A more powerful pull/push can be obtained by rolling the body by up to 40 degrees when pulling, bringing into play the powerful chest and back muscles. What is vitally important is that whatever roll and head movement is incorporated, the swimmer's head and body must re-centralize. A very common fault in Front Crawl for the competitive swimmer is to stay tipped over on the breathing side with a consequent less effective arm pull on the breathing side. The legs taper to a lower position than the hips when kicking.

Leg Action Propulsion is obtained from a strong down kick, with a plantar-flexed foot hitting the water with the front of the foot. Good ankle flexion giving a good plantar foot-flexion is essential in Front Crawl. The propulsive force of the Front Crawl kick can and has been measured, but the assistance to propulsion when swimming full stroke is believed to be negligible. The role of the leg kick at speed is basically stabilization. The textbook tells us that a six-beat leg kick is required, but modern coaching uses a four-beat or two-beat as the competition demands, some swimmers using a six-beat kick over short distances. (The theory of this is that the large leg and thigh muscles can use up glycogen reserves very rapidly, therefore depriving the propulsive chest muscles of energy.)

My squad are coached to think ballistically when swimming Front Crawl. When the right arm recovers the right leg should kick down to balance, and similarly with the left leg. The depth of kick is around 12 inches with action from the hip and some knee bend. Encourage kicking in any plane when teaching Front Crawl (that is, on the stomach or either side), because this will encourage the ability to retain a kick and body-roll combination when later development of the stroke is reached.

Arm Action The arm action is alternate as in Backstroke, but there is a fair amount of 'catch-up' involved in the arm action, which depends on the individual style and characteristic of the swimmer. This means the recovering arm will be well on its way to entry before the other arm has completed its pull/push. Hand entry should be palm down on a line between the shoulder and head. Hand exit is at the thigh.

The hands will, of course, alter their angle with the forearm, as the pull/push occurs in order to preserve the path of action towards the feet. All connected, as mentioned before, with water feel, and action and reaction being equal and opposite. An effective catch-point is again vital to good propulsion and catch should be made on, or just below, water surface. The path of the hand through the water, when viewed vertically from above the swimmer, from entry to exit can be best described as an 'inverted question mark'. (Counsilman's *Science of Swimming* 52.)

This path of pull/push is developed by the swimmer endeavouring to pull down the body centre-line and incorporating a bent-arm pull with body roll. The majority of swimmers are taught to pull with a bent arm on Front Crawl, and to keep the elbow high both in recovery and propulsion.

Breathing When to breathe is important. In-breath should not be taken until the hand on the opposite side to the breathing side has found catch-point and is pulling. Re-centralize the body and head in time to see the breathing arm enter at catch-point.

The mouth must be low in the water even when breathing. Breathe in the 'trough' formed in the water by the forehead.

It is of great importance to have a breathing pattern in Front Crawl—particularly over short distances. The first 50 metres of a 100-metre race can be swum with intermittent breathing to a definite plan, the second 50 metres with breathing at every stroke. Every individual swimmer should have his own pattern, but it should be a repetitive pattern.

The distances are usually swum breathing at every stroke after the first 50 metres, although some top competitors have set world records over 800-metre distances breathing bilaterally. My squad are coached to vary their breathing during the preparation period—changing their breathing side completely to the opposite side as required to encourage versatility and help eradicate faults.

Timing There is no timing as such in Front Crawl. The swimmer aims at a tremendously repetitive and rhythmical arm action with a varying amount of 'catch-up'. Generally the right leg kicks down as the right arm recovers, to balance the effect of a limb out of water, and vice versa with the left. The number of leg kicks per arm cycle is variable to each swimmer.

Chapter 9

The Swimming Training: General

In common with all other motor sports (those involving physical muscular movement) in swimming the technique must be learned correctly from the outset. It is believed that initial new physical movements, such as the learning of a skill like swimming, are activated from the brain at conscious or cerebral cortex level. At first the movements are unsure, unco-ordinated, slow and unrhythmical. As practice progresses, the movements become more polished, more assured, more co-ordinated and free of tension. The movement patterns when this stage is reached are almost certainly controlled no longer at the conscious level, but by the lower central nervous system at automatic level. There is a strong basis of fact supporting the theory that we have a memory storage drum of motor patterns at both cerebral cortex and automatic level. Thus we can see that a bad fault in swimming technique learnt initially can be continually drawn from the storage drum at automatic level without ever being altered, because the swimmer is not reverting to conscious level to correct it. Therefore we must learn all the strokes correctly when young to avoid carrying forward the bad habits of incorrect strokes.

Most modern coaches believe in training youngsters as early as possible, when the emphasis will be on mastering the techniques. The distances will be short initially, but as technique is mastered the distances should be increased as long as technique holds together. It will be no surprise therefore to find coaches with eight- and nine-year-olds whose swimming ability covers all strokes and whose training can include 2,000-metre swims on mixed strokes—1,500 metres Front Crawl, 800 metres Individual Medley, 800 metres Front Crawl, 400 metres on all strokes and 200 metres on all strokes. Their speed performance at this stage should be secondary to technique and yardage.

The amount of training a swimmer should do, as ability and performance begin to emerge at the onset of a swimming career, is entirely dependent on the individual. It depends on many things: psychology of approach to training, the physiological state of the swimmer at any period of time, the available facilities, the times of such facilities, the ambition of the swimmer, the parental interest, the atmosphere and other distractions of home life and the conflict of other interests. The amount of training should, and will, vary as do the above circumstances.

My squad are encouraged to build up to a minimum weekly distance of about 40,000 yards, (36,000 metres), which is possible by attending all our facilities plus morning training. Obviously if your evening sessions finish late, then morning training would be of questionable value if it deprives the younger swimmer of sleep. In such circumstances extra yards can be gained by additional midday training, in the school lunch hour if possible. My facilities end at the latest by 8.45 p.m. in summer and 8.30 p.m. in winter so that morning training fits in fairly well.

As a coach you will be responsible for deciding all matters on your squad's training and weekly yardage. You will have to decrease yardage perhaps when a teenage swimmer is experiencing accelerated growth rate and feeling tired. Similarly where homework is heavy and causing tiredness and fatigue—brainwork can be as exhausting as physical exercise to some children—you will again have to decide on a suitable amount of work for an individual. Lack of energy and poor performance in training has always been noticeable to me as a coach when young swimmers change from elementary school to a senior school. The training has to be adjusted to cater for these natural but upsetting influences. Some swimmers obtain a boost psychologically by achieving high yardage in training, but others can be just the opposite and still be in no way inferior in performance in competition.

The Swimming Training: General

Bearing all the above points in mind, I believe the system involved in my squad concerning attendance is better than most others because it is flexible. We do not insist on full attendance; swimmers are asked and advised what sessions they intend to attend at the onset of the season and then they are expected to adhere to them.

To all aspiring swimming coaches it should be made quite clear that hard training does not necessarily make national champions. Some training has to be hard, but not all the time. A squad training session should contain work of varying intensity because no human being can maintain high effort over too long a period. There are swimmers who achieve better times in training than they do in competition. Some swimmers are very predictable in training, some are quite inconsistent. Persevere with the inconsistent ones, the unpredictable ones, because my experience has shown that generally these are the types who thrive on competition and go on to become national champions.

However, as has already been stated, hard work is necessary, but not continuously. Bearing this in mind, therefore, you will find that progress in performance is only achieved by hard work for a period of time. You as a coach will be responsible for arranging a yearly programme of training, which on occasions will push your squad into periods of hard effort. Only by going into the hurt/pain region for a period, and then being brought out of it at the right moment of time by less-effort work, will a swimmer emerge at his major competition in good form. Should you as coach work him too hard and too long up to his competition, then you will get a jaded performance. Should you not work him hard enough or long enough up to his competition, then he will only reproduce his previous form.

Should all your squad generally be doing poor times in competition, be lackadaisical in training, grumbling about swimming training, then look to yourself, coach, or your methods or schedules with regard to variety of work or intensity of work.

Where facilities and time allow, all training should be preceded by a suitable warm-up, particularly in the competitive period. Even where water time is limited a little imagination can include a warm-up of sorts in your schedules, and still allow for valuable water work. Where you may have different groups coming in to a bath while a previous group is still working, remember that useful stretching/mobility exercises can be done while waiting.

From questions which I am frequently asked by young swimmers who are just starting their swimming careers, their parents, and also those who have had more experience in some cases, there appears to me to be some confusion and worry still in the minds of less experienced swimmers and parents regarding the amount of yardage and the intensity of work which should be done in training. The foregoing interpretation of the requirements will, I hope, give a better idea to all concerned of how to apply them to each individual case.

Additionally, one frequently hears swimmers and parents talking of 'tapering', or the 'taper period', and again I feel that there is a lack of communication on this particular subject. My interpretation of tapering is the deliberate reduction in weekly yardage by a swimmer prior to a major competition in order to allow maximum performance to emerge through partial rest. It is my opinion that only swimmers averaging 80,000 yards (73,000 metres) a week can be allowed to accommodate a legitimate taper as defined above.

My squad average around 40,000 yards (36,000 metres) weekly *and do not taper as such* prior to major competition. The work content becomes more specific—yardage will decrease slightly because of longer rest and increased starts/turns practice and that is as far as it goes. Our training is planned on general lines covering all strokes. As a major competition approaches, the work becomes more specific and swimmers concentrate more on their intended stroke and distance in that competition. The squad works very hard in the period preceding the competition and then, immediately prior to it, a lot of the pressure work is exchanged for work of a general nature with only a percentage of hard intensity working retained.

The Swimming Training: General

The closest approach to a legitimate taper by my squad is during school holidays when we obtain additional midday facilities. We have used these facilities for the National Championships and National Age Groups as an intensified training course preceding these events. Weekly yardage has been boosted to 60,000 yards (55,000 metres) or more (instead of 40,000) in the period prior to the competition and then eased off in the week before, with good results for most of the squad.

There also appears to be some confusion among parents, swimmers and intending coaches regarding the type of training to be done in the periods of the year. My squad does not stick rigidly to the preparation, pre-competitive and competitive type of yearly training programme as has been advocated in the past.

The swimming year for my squad can be described as follows:

PREPARATION PERIOD (About September to January depending on the proximity of the first major championships.)

Maximum of land conditioning (three sessions a week), maximum of yardage (this means predominance given to Front Crawl, Butterfly and Backstroke with less to Breast Stroke), short-rest swimming to develop stamina and endurance, maximum of stroke technique work (within reason so as not to hinder yardage target) ranging from altering breathing sides on Front Crawl to all other aspects of stroke technique (including hand paddle work to exaggerate already existing faults). Roughly the work divides out to about 80 per cent overdistance, stamina and endurance type of work with 20 per cent speed work.

COMPETITION PERIOD (Approximately February to August.)

Reduction in land conditioning (two sessions a week). Omit

land conditioning in the week prior to the major competition. The swimming rest periods increase (the nearer the major competition the more the rest periods increase).
(*Note:* My squad do not generally at any time have any greater rest when training than a 120-pulse beat).

Some reduction in technique work (breathing patterns for all strokes should now be established).

The introduction of swimming at *even pace* over distance events, the work dividing out to approximately 50 per cent speed and 50 per cent over distance, stamina and endurance type of work (again all dependent on proximity of major competition).

My squad works on a variable pattern of training in this period. For example, on Sundays and Mondays we would revert to preparation type of work, but as the week proceeded we would develop the training as outlined in the competitive period depending on what major competition was ahead. At periods in the competition season we revert to preparation type work for complete weeks in a 'yardage booster'. All such training is dictated by the diary of competition, when the major events occur. As mentioned previously, during school holidays my squad receive additional midday facilities where existing yardages can be almost doubled. These sessions can be used as yardage boosters prior to major competition where the timing is correct. The main effort work for the day is done at midday, with general yardage/technique work being done at night, or vice versa.

As a conclusion to general swimming training then, let us remember that all swimmers are not identical and nor are the coaches. As an aspiring swimming coach, you must become an individual. My experience over the years has led me to believe that the above training patterns and sequences are the most suitable and my squad's performances have improved. You will have to build up your own experiences through both fortune and misfortune and determine your own patterns and beliefs. The main thing in swimming (or any other sport for that matter, and in all aspects of life) is that you must not copy or follow others' advice without fully knowing and digesting

The Swimming Training: General

the reasons for so doing. No one should be silly enough to copy a practice simply because the Australians or the Americans do it, for example.

Know the reason for, or the theory behind, training methods and if you agree with them adopt them by all means. Then, if you are asked *why* do you do so and so, you can answer effectively without appearing an idiot.

Chapter 10

The Swimming Training: Specific

The following types of training all have their use in swimming schedules. The terms are explained, and also how such types of training are used in the schedules of my own squad. The first paragraphs are given to the teaching, or learning, of how to swim distance events at *even pace*, because there does not appear to be a lot of evidence that it is being coached as widely as it should be, judging by performances at District and National Championships.

PACING (SWIMMING A DISTANCE EVENT AT EVEN PACE)

The value of swimming at even pace in a distance race can be better illustrated by considering the hypothetical performance of two swimmers, A and B, in a 400-metre Front Crawl race, with the appropriate splits as shown.

	100 metres	200 metres	300 metres	400 metres
Swimmer A	72 sec. (split 72)	2 min.26 (split 74)	3 min.40 (split 74)	4 min.53 (split 73)
Swimmer B	69 sec. (split 69)	2 min.24 (split 75)	3 min.41 (split 77)	4 min.54 (split 73)

Swimmer A can be said to have swum at even pace and, in so doing, have swum a more economical race than B. Swimmer A would not have experienced the stress to which swimmer B subjected himself and would have finished the race in far better physical shape than B.

The Swimming Training: Specific

Swimmer B did not swim at even pace. For equivalent finishing times the first 100 metres was too fast, causing an energy drop in the middle of the race which had to be pulled back in the final 100 metres. A miscalculation of this sort in an 800-metre or 1,500-metre race could be calamitous.

My squad have available during training an even-pace chart, which shows all the racing distances on all strokes (excluding Medley) as a range of times for each event. These start at a standard for District Championships, finishing as a world record. These event times, which are listed at, say, 30-second stages, are further broken down to give the 100-metre and 50-metre associated pace times of such component distances, as would add up to the total event.

For example, part of an even-pace chart for the 800-metre Freestyle event would be as follows:

Target time 800 metres Freestyle	16 ×50–metre repeats	8 × 100–metre repeats
12 min.00 sec.	45 75.00 sec.	1 min.30.00 sec.
11 min.30 sec.	43.125 sec.	1 min.26.25 sec.
11 min.00 sec.	41.25 sec.	1 min.22.50 sec.
10 min.30 sec.	39.375 sec.	1 min.18.75 sec.
10 min.00 sec.	37.50 sec.	1 min.15.00 sec.

The pace charts are invaluable checks for experienced swimmers who may be asked to swim at their fastest 1,500-metre pace Freestyle for 25 minutes—the repeats to be 50 metres, rest interval 9 seconds. A quick check on the pace chart will give the 50-metre time required to give the overall target time.

Obviously less experienced swimmers can be confused by such a schedule and my squad learn to swim and accustom themselves to training at even pace as follows:

PREPARATION PERIOD

Swim 1,500 metres Freestyle timed on the clock, rest interval 80 seconds; then swim 15 × 100-metre Freestyle repeats, rest interval 12 seconds, where each 100 metres must equal the first 1,500-metre time divided by 15.

COMPETITIVE PERIOD

Swim 1,500 metres Freestyle timed on the clock, rest interval 2 minutes; then swim 15 × 100-metre Freestyle repeats, rest interval 12 seconds, where each 100 metres must equal the first 1,500-metre time divided by 15, minus 2 seconds.

COMPETITION PERIOD

Swim at your fastest 1,500-metre pace for 25 minutes—repeats are 100 metres, rest interval 12 seconds. (The swimmer obtains his target time by looking up his personal best on the pace chart.)

COMPETITION PERIOD

Swim at your fastest 1,500-metre pace for 25 minutes—repeats are 50 metres, rest interval 9 seconds. (The swimmer obtains his target time by looking up his personal best on the pace chart.)

Obviously the length of time you ask them to swim at their fastest pace depends on their current best times over the distance and the multiple rest periods added up.

As the major competition approaches (about one week before) we reduce the pacing to the actual distance, for example, 30 × 50-metre repeats, rest interval 9 seconds, to allow the fullest potential to develop.

An additional method of learning even-pace swimming, would be to include a set of repeats at the fastest pace on one day in the week's training, to be followed on the subsequent day in the same week by a straight swim, where the memory of the previous day's pace has to be recalled and simulated in the straight swim.

The above examples show only 1,500 metres Front Crawl but of course pacing can be applied to all other strokes (excluding Medley) such as 400 metres Front Crawl, 200 metres Backstroke, 200 metres Butterfly, etc.

Obviously Individual Medley races are not swum at even pace, but swimmers of such races have to be actively aware of their own current split times on all the 'legs' of the race.

SECTIONAL WORK

This term refers to leg kicking, arm pulling, the use of hand paddles, one-arm swimming, etc. The majority of sectional work is probably done in the preparation period as such, but remember that yardage is the primary target in this period.

My squad use small amounts of kicking-pulling and one-arm swimming as stroke technique preliminary work which again could lead up to a set of repeats.

For example, single-arm swimming on Front Crawl, Butterfly and Backstroke can be useful in aiding correct feel for the water, good hand positioning throughout the pull/push. Single-arm Backstroke swims can be usefully used to encourage turning on both left and right arms in turn. Hand paddles can be used to correct incorrect hand positions; here again, all the paddle does is illustrate more clearly to the coach and possibly the swimmer that slip is occurring. The actual correction must come from the brain of the swimmer. Distances on leg kicking (e.g. 200- or 300-metre swims) I use solely for loosening, or technique, or variety between repeats. For toughening up of leg muscles and strengthening the leg kick, we do shorter distances—wave 25 metres or 50 metres working as hard as possible against a partner, or 3 × 100 metres reducing the time on each. Breast-strokers on my squad always kick a longer distance than their fellows on the other strokes.

We also use sectional work in conjunction with varied distances and also fartlek (varied speed) work. For example:

Kick—1 length—2 length—3 length—4 length—3 length—2

length—1 length, where the 1 length would be done on the No. 4 kick, the 2 lengths on the No. 3 kick, the 3 lengths on the No. 1 kick and the 4 lengths on the No. 2 kick.

The preceding example could be varied on occasions by doing the worst kick on the longer length swims, and the best kick on the 1 lengths. The same example could again be varied by doing the complete set on the No. 1 kick, but the odd-number lengths to be done slow or easy pace, with the even-number lengths being done faster.

My squad also use the following type of build-up on all strokes and distances quite frequently:

Kick 100 metres Backstroke, rest interval 15 seconds.

Swim 100 metres Backstroke right arm only, turning on right arm, rest interval 15 seconds.

Swim 100 metres Backstroke left arm only, turning on left arm, rest interval 15 seconds.

Swim 4 × 200 metres Backstroke checking arm timing, rest interval 30 seconds.

SLOW INTERVAL

A term given to a set of repeat swims which have only short rests between. (The 'slow' refers to the speed of the repeats, which would not be fast because of the short rest periods.) For example: 4 × 200 metres Breast Stroke, rest interval 25 seconds. This type of work would be used predominantly in the preparation period.

My squad use slow interval work in both the preparation and the competitive periods. Rest intervals are in the order of, say, 4 × 400 metres Front Crawl or Individual Medley, rest interval 50 seconds; 8 × 200 metres, rest interval 25 seconds; 16 × 100 metres going every 2 minutes. We frequently do a set of 50 metres on all strokes going every 50 seconds, 55 seconds or 60 seconds dependent on lane ability.

The main purpose of this type of training is to improve stamina, endurance and some technique work. Speed training is also involved in the 50-metre type of work.

The Swimming Training: Specific

FAST INTERVAL (the opposite of slow interval)

A term given to a set of repeats which have a longer period of rest between each repeat. ('Fast' refers to the speed of the swim which will be fast as opposed to slow, because of the increased rest period.) For example: 4 × 200 metres Breast Stroke, rest interval 70 seconds. This type of work is used predominantly in the competition period.

My squad use fast interval work as above. The work could entail 4 × 400 metres Front Crawl, rest interval 80 seconds; 4 × 200 metres, rest interval 60 seconds, 4 × 100 metres going on 3 minutes; 4 × 100 metres going on 2½ minutes; 16 × 50 metres going on 1½ minutes, etc.

OVER DISTANCE

A term applied in swimming training, where, for a swimmer specifically training for a 400-metre event, for example, any distance trained on above this would be termed 'over-distance'. Work of this type is very neglected in the competitive period. Stamina and endurance gained from over-distance work is more stable and longer lasting than that gained from short-distance, short-rest repeats.

My squad use over-distance all year round. As previously mentioned, week-ends are over-distance sessions for us all year round. We train over all the distances—1,500 metres Front Crawl, 800 metres Front Crawl, 400 metres Front Crawl, 200 metres Front Crawl, etc., 800 metres Individual Medley, 400 metres Individual Medley, 200 metres Individual Medley, 400 metres Backstroke, 200 metres Backstroke, 400 metres Butterfly, 200 metres Butterfly, 400 metres Breast Stroke, 200 metres Breast Stroke.

We do swims of 2,000 metres or more on occasions, but these are usually built up from various strokes such as 400 metres Front Crawl, 400 metres Backstroke, 400 metres Front Crawl, 400 metres Backstroke, 400 metres Front Crawl to avoid monotony and boredom.

FARTLEK

A term applied to training where variation of speed is deliberately used within a swim or set of repeats. A useful method of helping to teach speed impressions or water feel, also very useful as variational work between hard phases of training. Can be usefully employed both in the preparation and competition periods. For example: swim 400 metres Backstroke, each alternate 50 metres to be swum slow/faster.

My squad use fartlek training as outlined above and we apply it to all types of training on occasions. For example, in sectional work we may kick 200 metres No. 1 stroke, alternate 25 metres to be swum slow/faster, or we may kick or pull a 1 length/2 lengths, 3 lengths/4 lengths/3 lengths/2 lengths/1 length where the odd number lengths 1 and 3 will be done slow and the even number lengths 2 and 4 will be done faster. We may use fartlek in distance work such as 800 metres Front Crawl, where each alternate 100 metres will be done slow/faster. We also use fartlek, or speed play, on sets of slow or fast interval 50 metres. We swim 50 metres *hard* going on 50 seconds for 12 minutes, then the next 5 minutes is a partial recovery swim doing 50 metres, rest interval 8 seconds, at own speed to re-obtain the correct stroke (I call this 'freewheeling'), finally reverting to 12 minutes doing 50 metres *hard* on 50 seconds again.

REPETITIONS

A term much confused in swimming. The true sense of the term is a set of repeated shorter distances than the competition distance for which the swimmer is training. These are used in the competition period, mainly where more complete heart recovery is given between repeats. For example: for a swimmer training for a 100-metre race—12 × 50 metres going on $1\frac{1}{2}$ minutes or 2 minutes.

My squad use repetitions in their swimming curriculum, but

we do not employ them in their more ideal sense. We do sets of 50-metre repeats where the maximum rest ever used is probably going every 2 minutes. The majority are done every 1½ minutes but we also do 50 metres going every 1¼ minutes, 1 minute or 50 seconds, dependent on stroke and the ability of the various lanes. The maximum we do is probably 20 × 50-metre repeats but usually the 16 × 50 metres, adding up to the half-mile approximately, is more widely used. We also combine 50 metres into a set of 100-metre repeats on occasions, on all strokes, where a typical schedule would be: swim 12 × alternate 50-metre and 100-metre repeats going every 2 minutes and 3 minutes where the target is to keep the 100-metre times within the preceding 50-metre time multiplied by 2, plus 3 or 4 seconds. For example: No. 1 repeat, 50 metres on zero; No. 2 repeat, 100 metres on 2 minutes; No. 3 repeat, 50 metres on 5 minutes; No. 4 repeat, 100 metres on 7 minutes, etc., up to 12 repeats. We do quite a lot of 50-metre repeats in the preparation period which helps retain a little sharpness combined with stamina/endurance, but all are done on short rest intervals.

SPRINTS

A term given to all-out effort swims over short distances where more complete heart recovery is given. Most usually used in the competition period. For example: swim 12 ×33⅓ metres from dive, rest interval 120 pulse. My squad use a certain amount of sprints, although we do them in both the competition and preparation periods.

In the preparation period my squad do 25-metre or 33⅓-metre sprints to retain a little sharpness, association with starts and dives, but the rest intervals are short. In the competition period more rest is given to allow greater effort and speed to be produced. When my squad use this type of work we always climb out of the bath by arm power only, not using the legs, so that we combine a little strength work with them.

REPEATS

A general term referring to a series of swims in any swimming training schedule. They can be slow interval, fast interval, sprints, repetitions, etc. *Note:* Many people refer in their swimming vocabulary to 'repetitions', when in the true sense of the word they mean 'repeats'.

STRAIGHT REPEATS

As above, a general term referring to a series of swims in a swimming schedule of training, but in this instance all the repeats are of the same distance. Can be used in both the preparation and competition periods. Example 10 × 100 metres. My squad use straight repeats in their training schedules. In fact, for a session where only limited time is available, you will not go far astray with a 10 × 100 metres set of repeats. Beware of the boredom aspect of straight repeats, however. At one time, when coaching played 'follow the leader', everyone was competing against everyone in the number of straight repeats they could do. It was reported in one journal that one squad used 100 × 100 metres repeats. The maximum number of straight repeats my squad do (in the true sense of the term) is roughly of the following order: 3 × 800 metres Front Crawl or 4 × 400 metres Front Crawl or Individual Medley or 12 × 200 metres or 20 × 100 metres or 30 × 50 metres.

We vary rest intervals when doing such work, depending on preparation or competitive periods. We do a greater number of repeats than those shown above on occasions, but the pattern of work is altered slightly to relieve boredom. For example, we may do 2 × 1,500 metres Front Crawl, but the second repeat would be broken into 15 × 100 metres, rest interval 12 seconds, where the target would be to equal the first 1,500 metres time divided by 15 on each 100 metres.

We do a lot of 100-metre repeats where every alternate 100

The Swimming Training: Specific

metres is divided into 2 × 50 metres, rest interval 10 seconds, the target being to beat each preceding straight 100-metre time on the broken swim. We use this at the end of the preparation period to awaken dormant speed; we also use this work in the competition period.

Another alternative to relieve boredom in straight repeats is to alter stroke. For example: 24 × 100-metre repeats going on $2\frac{1}{2}$ minutes, comprising 6 × 100 metres Butterfly, 6 × 100 metres Backstroke, 6 × 100 metres Breast Stroke, 6 × 100 metres Front Crawl, which may be done straight or with every alternate one broken, as previously outlined.

My squad use similar tactics on all distances. For example: 6 × 400 metres Individual Medleys, rest interval 70 seconds, each alternate 400 metres broken into 4 × 100 metres, rest interval 12 seconds, where the target is again to beat each preceding straight swim time on the broken one.

One can also vary rest periods in straight repeats. My squad vary rest periods even in the competitive period. For example, we may do 6 × 100 metres going on 3 minutes, 6 × 100 metres on $2\frac{1}{2}$ minutes, 6 × 100 metres on 2 minutes, as a complete set of straight repeats. Obviously the first six repeats will be genuinely done, while the following twelve repeats will be accepted more as conditioning swims.

DECREASING DISTANCE

A term referring to a set of repeats where the distance swum on each repeat is reduced. A psychological encourager. For example, swim 400 metres Front Crawl, 300 metres Front Crawl, 200 metres Front Crawl, 100 metres Front Crawl, with rest intervals varying.

My squad incorporate a lot of decreasing-distance swims in their training. It is a very useful way of doing a large yardage on one stroke without introducing the boredom of a continuous swim. My experience has shown that with younger children, eight to nine or ten years old, a definite collapse of technique and interest can occur in a 3,000-metre Front Crawl swim.

Better technique and interest will be maintained by breaking up the work as follows:

Swim 800 metres Front Crawl, rest interval 70 seconds, timed.

Swim 600 metres Front Crawl, rest interval 60 seconds, must be done in three-quarters of 800-metre time.

Swim 400 metres Front Crawl, rest interval 50 seconds, must be done in half of 800-metre time.

Swim 200 metres Front Crawl, rest interval 40 seconds, must be done in a quarter of 800-metre time.

The result is 2,000 yards Front Crawl swum at the same pace. Rest intervals are variable depending on the period of the swimming year.

In a similar manner, my squad would train to do a certain yardage on the other strokes in a decreasing-distance pattern of work as follows:

Swim 400 metres Butterfly, rest interval 70 seconds, timed.

Swim 300 metres Butterfly, rest interval 60 seconds, must be done in three-quarters of 400-metre time.

Swim 200 metres Butterfly, rest interval 50 seconds, must be done in half of 400-metre time.

Swim 100 metres Butterfly, rest interval 40 seconds, must be done in one-quarter of 400-metre time.

This also can be done on Backstroke, Breast Stroke or Medley. Again the rest intervals would be variable dependent on the particular phase of the swimming year.

My squad have also included the following in their workouts:

Swim 800 metres Front Crawl, rest interval 80 seconds, timed.

Swim 700 metres Front Crawl, rest interval 70 seconds, must be swum in the split 700-metre time from the 800-metre swim.

Swim 600 metres Front Crawl, rest interval 60 seconds, must be swum in the split 600-metre time from the 700-metre swim.

Swim 500 metres Front Crawl, rest interval 50 seconds, must

be swum in the split 500-metre time from the 600-metre swim.

Swim 400 metres Front Crawl, rest interval 40 seconds, must be swum in the split 400-metre time from the 500-metre swim.

Swim 300 metres Front Crawl, rest interval 30 seconds, must be swum in the split 300-metre time from the 400-metre swim.

Swim 200 metres Front Crawl, rest interval 20 seconds, must be swum in the split 200-metre time from the 300-metre swim.

Total 3,500 metres Front Crawl swum at approximately the same pace.

SIMULATORS

A term given to broken swims or split swims in swimming training. Predominantly used in the competitive season. The swim more closely approximates to the actual stress and effort produced in competition than any other form of swimming training, yet avoids the actual sustained effort required over the unbroken racing distance. For example: swim 100 metres simulator, No. 1 stroke, broken into 2 × 50 metres, rest interval 10 seconds.

My squad use simulators in their schedules both in the competition period and the latter part of the preparation period over all distances and strokes.

We use them either 'in bulk' to encourage increased speed, or singly to try to beat a personal best time. For example: 1 × 800 metres Front Crawl, timed, rest interval 2 minutes, then swim 8 × 100 metres Front Crawl, rest interval 12 seconds. The total time for these 100 metres must add up to better than the straight 800-metre time.

We may do 10 × 100 metres No. 1 stroke going every 2½ minutes. Each alternate 100 metres will be broken into 2 × 50 metres, rest interval 10 seconds, where the target is to beat the preceding straight swim time on each simulator—No. 1 repeat (straight)—No. 2 repeat (broken)—No. 3 repeat (straight) —No. 4 repeat (broken), etc.

As a single test of speed where it is used in its truest sense, my squad use the simulator once in a session, and as a good time is required it is used early on in the training session after a useful warm-up. For example:

Warm-up—kick 50 metres—swim 50 metres—kick 50 metres—swim 50 metres No. 1 stroke easy pace, rest interval 30 seconds.

Warm-up—swim 200 metres No. 1 stroke easy pace but going faster into and out of all turns, rest interval 30 seconds.

Warm-up—3 × 50 metres No. 1 stroke going on 1½ minutes and reducing times to 85 per cent effort.

Warm-up—swim 3 × 1 length No. 1 stroke checking starts and reducing to 85 per cent effort.

Then on a lower than 120 pulse beat, swim 1 × 100 metres simulator No. 1 stroke—broken into 2 × 50 metres—rest interval 12 seconds. Target: beat personal best time for 100 metres.

MIXED SETS (HUNGARIAN REPEATS)

A term given to a set of repeats embodying varying distances and strokes, thus giving variety and relief from boredom. It is also another way of doing 'yardage' where short rest periods are used and useful work in building up all strokes for Medley swimming is provided. For example: swim 4 × 100 metres, 3 × 200 metres, 2 × 400 metres, 1 × 800 metres, 2 × 400 metres, 3 × 200 metres, 4 × 100 metres.

My squad include this kind of work in their schedules, mainly in the preparation period although on occasions in the competitive period such work could be used depending on the immediate objective. As well as varying stroke and distance in the repeats, we may also include sectional work such as this: kick 1 length, 2 lengths, 3 lengths, 4 lengths, 3 lengths, 2 lengths, 1 length. The 1 lengths on the No. 4 kick, the 2 lengths

The Swimming Training: Specific

on the No. 3 kick, the 3 lengths on the No. 1 kick and the 4 lengths on the No. 2 kick. (On occasions reverse the order so that the maximum distance is kicked on the worst kick, etc.) The above can be repeated doing arm pulling and then full stroke if necessary.

Two typical examples of a full training session on mixed sets are as follows:

- 6 × 50 metres Butterfly, rest interval 20 seconds.
- 6 × 100 metres (3 on Butterfly, 3 on Breast Stroke), rest interval 25 seconds.
- 3 × 200 metres No. 1 stroke, rest interval 30 seconds.
- 2 × 400 metres (1 on Individual Medley, 1 on Front Crawl), rest interval 50 seconds.
- 1 × 800 metres Front Crawl, rest interval 70 seconds.
- 2 × 400 metres (1 on Front Crawl, 1 on Individual Medley), rest interval 50 seconds.
- 3 × 200 metres No. 1 stroke, rest interval 30 seconds.
- 6 × 100 metres (3 on Backstroke, 3 on Front Crawl), rest interval 25 seconds.
- 6 × 50 metres Breast Stroke, rest interval 20 seconds.

Note: Rests can vary according to the objective, and the strokes can also vary, depending on various lane abilities. For example:

- 6 × 50 metres Butterfly, rest interval 20 seconds.
- 6 × 100 metres No. 1 stroke, rest interval 25 seconds.
- 3 × 200 metres (1 on Butterfly, 1 on Backstroke, 1 on Individual Medley), rest interval 30 seconds.
- 2 × 400 metres Front Crawl, rest interval 50 seconds.
- 1 × 800 metres Front Crawl, rest interval 70 seconds.
- 2 × 400 metres Front Crawl, rest interval 50 seconds.
- 3 × 200 metres (1 on Breast Stroke, 1 on Front Crawl, 1 on Individual Medley), rest interval 30 seconds.
- 6 × 100 metres No. 1 stroke, rest interval 25 seconds.
- 6 × 50 metres Breast Stroke, rest interval 20 seconds.

The rest interval can again be variable, also the strokes, as applicable to lane, ability, etc.

PROGRESSIVE SETS (REDUCING TIME SWIMS)

A term given to a set of repeats where the speed of each successive swim increases. Basically used in the competitive period, but also used in the preparation period, particularly at the latter end to rekindle and awaken dormant speed. For example: swim 4 × 100 metres progressive, the swims progressively faster up to No. 4.

Reducing swims are included in my schedules on all strokes and in both periods of training. The work may cover all distances. We may on occasions do practically a complete training session on reducing type of work. Remember, however, that only swimmers of some experience will efficiently handle this type of work so, in the beginning with your squad, keep the number of repeats to be done to a minimum, thus:

Swim 3 × 400 metres Front Crawl, rest interval 50 seconds, reduce to 85 per cent effort minimum on No. 3.

Swim 4 × 100 metres No. 1 stroke going on 2½ minutes, reduce to fastest on No. 4.

Swim 3 × 100 metres going on 2½ minutes and reduce to fastest on No. 3, then swim 4 × 100 metres going on 2½ minutes and hold the time on No. 3.

Swim 2 × 800 metres Front Crawl, rest interval 60 seconds, No. 2 repeat to be the fastest, where No. 1 becomes a below-pace technique/turns swim.

Swim 2 × 200 Backstroke, rest interval 20 seconds, No. 2 repeat to be the fastest, where No. 1 becomes a below-pace technique swim.

The following schedule of repeats can be used to bring all the strokes into action on a progressive set basis:

Swim 3 × 400 metres Front Crawl, rest interval 50 seconds, No. 1 easier, No. 2 reduce to 85 per cent minimum effort, No. 3 hold No. 2 time.

Swim 3 × 200 metres Backstroke, rest interval 30 seconds, No. 1 easier, No. 2 reduce to 85 per cent minimum effort, No. 3 hold No. 2 time.

Swim 3 × 200 metres, rest interval 30 seconds, No. 1 easier,

The Swimming Training: Specific

No. 2 reduce to 85 per cent minimum effort, No. 3 hold No. 2 time. (No. 1 stroke out of Butterfly or Breast Stroke.) Swim 3 × 100 metres, rest interval 20 seconds, No. 1 easier, No. 2 reduce to 85 per cent minimum effort, No. 3 hold No. 2 time. (No. 2 stroke out of Butterfly or Breast Stroke.)

ALTERNATING PROGRESSIVE/REGRESSIVE SETS

A term referring to a set of repeats of varying speeds. Basically used in the competitive period and can be employed as useful variety work or a psychological reliever at the end of a hard phase of training.

My squad employ the above kind of work in their schedules, usually at the end of a hard phase of training. For example: swim 6 × 100 metres going on 2½ minutes, the odd-number repeats to be progressive and the even numbers regressive, or

No. 1	No. 2	No. 3	No. 4	No. 5	No. 6
Slow	Fast	Medium	Medium	Fast	Slow

Another added facet which we use is to make the same-effort swims identical in timing as in this example:

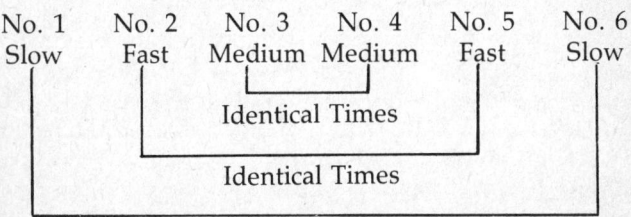

We have done similar work on 200-metre distance repeats, but to date have not tried any longer distance repeats. It would be interesting to see the kind of results obtained with a group of middle-distance swimmers on 400-metre repeats. All such work must obviously be done on the same stroke.

ALTERNATING FAST/SLOW SET

A term referring to a set of repeats where alternate repeats are swum faster or slower. More of a variety provider and psychological reliever, used in both the competition and preparation periods. For example:
  Swim 6 × 100 metres, alternate 100 metres swum fast/slower.

My squad use this kind of work in their schedules on all strokes, usually over the 100-metre and 50-metre distances.

The following type of schedule would be used at the end of a hard phase of training:
  Swim 6 × 100 metres No. 1 stroke going on $2\frac{1}{2}$ minutes, alternate 100 metres to be fast/slow.
  Swim 10 × 50 metres No. 1 stroke going on $1\frac{1}{2}$ minutes, alternate 50 metres to be fast/slow.

BROKEN SETS

Not currently a very widely used form of training, which is very unfortunate. Broken sets are a very good form of work to suit all types of swimmer because they are both speed producers and also stamina and endurance encouragers.

They can be used in both preparation and competition periods. My squad use quite a lot of this type of work in both training periods and also with some adaptations. For instance: swim 4 × 50 metres No. 1 stroke, rest interval 15 seconds. Maximum effort must be exerted on all repeats and the pattern of times is a first No. 1 repeat followed by successively slower 2nd, 3rd and 4th repeats as effort and short rest make their effect felt. Then swim 4 × 50 metres No. 1 stroke, rest interval 15 seconds, restarting on a 120 pulse. The second set of 4 × 50 metres must be done trying to achieve identical times with the first set. Rest until pulse is 120, then repeat a third set of 4 × 50 metres No. 1 stroke, trying to achieve identical times with the first set.

The Swimming Training: Specific

On occasions my squad adapt the foregoing and make it more competitive by partner work. Lanes are paired off on identical time basis. The swimmers work as a pair. The coach starts the initial set off on a 120 pulse at, say, 4-second intervals, but after that the winner of each 50-metre repeat counts the 15-second rest and shouts 'Go' to restart his partner. The winner is the swimmer successful in the most 50-metre repeats.

Chapter 11

The Swimming Coach

If you wish to be a successful swimming coach then you will have to become a very dedicated person, particularly if you are an amateur and do not receive payment for your labours.

The person required to take the blame for the failures of competitive swimmers is ultimately the coach, whether it be his fault or not.

If by nature you are a very sensitive person, then you may be in the wrong sport because you will have to hide your feelings on many occasions and learn to acquire a pretty tough skin.

Parents of competitive swimmers can be a nuisance to coaches because, even with the best will in the world, they frequently become critical and interfering and capable of 'knowing better than the coach'. Note that this statement is a general remark and in no way reflects on the many parents who do not fall into this category.

The coach cannot afford to ignore the parents, however, because there is much more to producing a swimming champion than just training a swimmer for two or three hours a day. As a coach you will only see the children for those limited periods a day when they train, and you will never know, unless you ask, what happens over the rest of the day—how they sleep, how long they sleep, how they are at school, how much homework they do, what they eat, when they eat, etc. In other words, you will require good relationships with parents to learn about and discuss all these other facts about your swimmers.

On some matters you may learn some things from your swimmers which parents do not know about their children's

The Swimming Coach

habits, desires or intentions, but generally the parents will have information which you will have to ask about.

You cannot hope to be perfect as a coach; you will come to realize this as you grow older and obtain greater experience. No one is perfect in any profession or sport. All swimming coaches have different and various personality attributes and varying degrees of skills. For example, some may hide a great coaching talent under an introvert personality, others may have a lesser coaching talent but an extrovert personality which attracts more attention. Some coaches have better coaching relationships with boys than with girls. Some coaches have great coaching motivation for Age Group swimmers rather than senior swimmers. Some coaches work magic with, say, two or three swimmers but fail with a squad of thirty swimmers. You will be very fortunate if you coach in a situation which suits perfectly the kind of category you fall into as a coach.

What you have to come to terms with are your own shortcomings or deficiencies as a coach and work to improve them as your experience develops.

A good swimming coach, or in any other sport for that matter, is one who is always learning. Beware of those who know it all.

When you plan a training schedule, whether it be for your top squad or lowest club group, it is a good idea to ask yourself these questions:

(1) What is its purpose?
(2) Would I have enjoyed doing it?
(3) Have they learnt anything?

Should you not obtain satisfactory answers to these questions, then revise and re-edit your schedule.

The first important step in coaching is to learn to control your squad. It is one thing to take an intermediate club group of ten swimmers for a half-hour session, and quite another to take an advanced squad of forty swimmers for a two-hour session.

Swimmers are no different from classes of schoolchildren. They will quickly discover *your* temperament as a teacher, although you are endeavouring to teach them. If they discover that they can work in a haphazard manner and get away with effort continually below what they should be doing, then I am afraid your squad will do just that!

You, as coach, must have discipline and you must motivate in them a will to work and the will to do things properly in training. You will not achieve this by wielding the big stick.

These results will only be achieved by establishing a trust and common knowledge between yourself and your swimmers that you know what you are doing and that what you are doing is right and producing good results.

Eventually in your squad, as happens in every other situation in life and sport, you will have to crack down on troublemakers. Try to do it between yourself and the person concerned and not in front of the whole squad. Unfortunately some children will deliberately go out to cause a confrontation between you as teacher and themselves in front of as big an audience as possible. Should this happen then your own experience and temperament have to make you appear the winner. There is plenty of room for a laugh in training as long as the work is done satisfactorily as well.

You will be required as a coach to push and motivate hard on occasions; and you must realize that a tense sarcastic comment from a tired swimmer as a result is not really intended but is part of the rigours of your job. In fact, as well as being a swimming coach you will have to develop as no mean psychologist and diplomat.

Every thinking coach must have a yearly plan. Draw up a week-by-week plan of the coming year's swimming activity—by this is meant the major competitions. The competitions are marked where it is important that the swimmers are at maximum fitness and speed.

Around this diary of events and times, now plan all the work schedules, the type of schedule and work effort required, for example, preparation period, competitive period, etc.

If you have a varied age and varied ability squad, then remember that endeavouring to bring swimmers to a peak of physical condition at a certain time is variable for Age Groupers as opposed to Seniors. A Senior, broadly speaking, is

The Swimming Coach

interested only in a good time at the National Short Course Championships and the National Championships, while an Age Group swimmer is interested basically in a qualifying time at County and District Level with a culmination of effort at the National Age Groups.

Unfortunately this can be made more complicated by Seniors selected for Internationals and other special events, and by better Age Group swimmers who are competing additionally in National Championships, Junior Internationals and Age Group Internationals. As a coach you must plan to suit the main competitions for your squad and ignore the minor ones. Here again, you may find yourself at opposing points of view with some parents, who believe it all important that their particular child must win everything.

At this point you must decide on the type of training you are going to aim for in the coming year, probably based on the previous year's experiences of successes and failures. My own squad do all types of work on all the strokes, so that in addition to doing their own No. 1 stroke on occasions, they will all train on the same stroke at the same time very frequently. All coaches should retain their yearly schedules as a cross-check on past performances, reasons for failures, etc. All schedules are best prepared a week in advance.

The reason for preparing schedules a week in advance is the obvious time-saving element to the coach. However, no coach should become so schedule minded that he fails to feel the mood or swim ability of his squad, and pushes them into schedules for which they are not in the mood. A coach who is not prepared to alter a schedule to ensure the compatibility of his squad on the bathside has a lot to learn.

As previously mentioned, you as coach, with your *planned* diary of yearly events, will be responsible for the timing of your *hard effort work* which will push your squad into the *pain/hurt concept* and then, with similar timing, relieve the stress by suitably planned schedules which will allow your swimmers to 'rebound' to a better-than-original form.

Additionally, as previously mentioned, should your whole squad be doing poor repeat times, poor competition times, grumbling generally about work, the length of the training sessions, etc., then beware, coach! Have a look at yourself, your schedules and in particular the variety element of your work.

Depending on the size of your squad or the size of the pool, you will in all probability need bathside assistants or lane coaches. Try to remember that these people, as well as your swimmers, will require guidance from you. In fact, if you have a professional coaching position it will almost certainly be part of your job to train assistant coaches. Obviously you require people who believe in the same training methods as yourself. Try to avoid using parents of swimmers as lane coaches, or, if you have to use parents, give them a lane which does not contain their own child. You will require a large *pace time clock*, which you will have to teach your beginners to read, and you should have an *even-pace chart* from which your swimmers can read and work out their pace times for swimming at even pace. A useful point to remember is to feel the pool water as you start the training. We occasionally, through mishaps, have too warm water, which means that schedules for that night may be better altered to something a little easier. Another most useful point to remember is that where your training is based continually on chain swimming in rotated lanes, the rotation of such lanes is better reversed every night to avoid the bad habits picked up in turning on the same hand for weeks on end.

Build up your own experiences. Do not copy other coaches unless you are well satisfied as to their methods and thoroughly understand the theory and reasons behind them. As stated previously, nothing shows up a fool more in any walk of life, than if, on being asked why he did a certain thing, he has to admit it was because he copied it from someone else.

Be punctual at sessions. If you require your swimmers to be diligent and on time, then you had better provide the good example. A major point which must be mentioned—please do not coach at all if you cannot make the effort to follow your swimmers up in competitions. Your coaching job is not fulfilled in any part until the competitive race of your swimmer is finished.

Try to have patience and understanding with your swimmers; the more zealous you are by nature that your swimmers should do well (which is a good thing), the more your patience and understanding will be tested to extremes on occasions. Try to remember occasionally that you are dealing with sportsmen who train purely for the love of the sport, with no monetary reward; that in itself deserves your forbearance because there are not many amateurs left in sport.

Chapter 12

The Swimming Competition

The presentation and format of swimming competitions, including the distances swum in galas, is now lagging far behind our present coaching and swimming ability standards. There is a lot to be learnt from overseas on types and format of competitions. The above remarks refer more particularly to the competitions organized by Club, County or District organizations and not to those organized by our governing body, the Amateur Swimming Association, at National level.

Generally speaking we are still following the old-established viewpoint that younger children of nine, ten and eleven years should race only over the shorter distances —25-metre, 50-metre, and 66⅔-metre events. This viewpoint is in my experience completely wrong and illogical. Where a young swimmer is able to master the distances involved and holds his stroke technique together, then he should be encouraged to compete on any distance. Certainly the young swimmer who has been introduced to all strokes and distances will carry on as age progresses and compete on all strokes and distances according to preference, but the swimmer who has always trained and competed over short distances will not easily transfer to longer distances at an older age.

At the present time we still have clubs and parents of competitors prepared to travel 200 miles to compete over a 25-metre, 33⅓-metre or 50-metre event in one competition. Schools' swimming competitions still offer very little in this field.

There is certainly a need for such competitions, but generally there are far too many of them compared to competitions over longer distances. Most coaches have now adapted their

The Swimming Competition

training programmes to cover all distances on all strokes for all ages, but where are the middle and long distance galas to be found for our younger, less experienced swimmers?

Apart from the field of competition, unfortunately there are still clubs and organizations where the training of young swimmers follows the same pattern—all training being short distance work and usually at too high an effort. How boring for the younger swimmers with no variation, and what a lack of education and opportunity to learn all the facets of swimming.

Additionally there is now available considerable scientific data which indicates that a varied-distance type of swimming training for younger swimmers is far more efficient. It produces a better type of cardiac system, particularly in relation to structure and wall thickness of the heart, than training which persists in short-distance work at high effort.

We place our young swimmers under too much stress at too many unimportant galas through the year. For example, in our current Age Group structure, we still have finals at County, District and National level. Finals should be eliminated from County and District galas of this sort and awards made from seeded heat times. After all the only object of entering these galas, surely, is to do a qualifying time to proceed up the ladder to the National event. Such a system would relieve the young swimmer from the pressures of winning at all costs at every gala, would cut down the length of the galas concerned and might also give the opportunity for longer distances to be swum.

Similarly our District Championships should be brought into line with these principles. Finals should be eliminated from our District Championships, all awards being made as a result of seeded heat times. Only at National Championships should the finals occur. This procedure would also give more time at District level for additional races and what is more important, it would provide additional heats and additional qualifiers. Our District Championships should also be run, as are the National events, with qualifying times stated for each event. It is highly gratifying to find some clubs who early each year put on an open gala incorporating practically the National programme to help swimmers to do qualifying times for the current year.

As a country we are still not giving our young swimmers enough experience of overseas competition. Great strides have been made in the right direction but it is still not enough.

Overseas competition should be introduced to our swimmers at eleven years. It would be of tremendous advantage to our youngsters if selected swimmers could accompany the older teams on occasions, purely for the experience. The first overseas trip involving travel, different climatic conditions, different foods, is more than enough for a newcomer to handle without the stress and psychological pressure of international competition in addition.

As mentioned in earlier chapters, all competition for the younger swimmer should be arranged to be *progressive*. An introduction to competition at Club level first could be a starting-off point, followed by the Schools' and the League galas and the County Age Groups. After this stage, there should be more individual competition, progressing to District and National Age Groups. Following on from these, as performance improves, the District and National Championships should be entered. Somewhere before this stage, all swimmers should have been abroad for experience in overseas competition, either with their club or with a national team or as an individual, even to International European Age Group Contests.

Parents should watch the competition aims of their children's swimming clubs closely, as is their right. A club which only competes in local galas and League swims will take a potential champion only part of the way. Where the standard of competition stays at the same level then the child's ambition will also tend to die out or be fixed on one level. One must have competition; there is no point in training competitively without having competition, but it is possible to have too much competition. This can interfere with training regularly and should be avoided. I believe that there is no point, either as a club or an individual, in competing at a gala without having a specific purpose or aim. Far too many invitations to galas are

The Swimming Competition

accepted purely for their social standing rather than as a sequence in a build-up of training as part of a yearly plan to bring a swimming squad up to peak performance.

Finally, a word to competitors about swimming competitions. If you compete in a gala, no matter where it may be or at whatever level of competition, then you should always give of your best. Even if, on current times, you may know before the race starts that you will win, I still believe you should win as easily and as speedily as you can. After all, although you are an amateur you are also an entertainer and competitor and the audience is entitled to your best possible performance. You should also acquire such a professional pride in your work that it will not allow you to give a slipshod performance, or, in other words, have your own personal standard of performance below which you will not allow yourself to fall.

Chapter 13

The Swimmer's Parents

Although I have stated in previous chapters that over-anxious parents result in more swimmers being lost to the sport than from any other cause and that parents on the bathside where their own children are training are to be avoided, I have nevertheless also said that all coaches should maintain the closest liaison with the parents of swimmers, if only for the reason that parents see much more of their children than the coach does.

Parents have the power to make or break a child's chance of becoming a national champion and, in my experience, a swimmer with uninterested parents may go a little of the way but will not make the top flight in swimming.

Therefore, parents, do not encourage your child to swim competitively unless you are prepared to give up your spare time to assist him as much as possible and never forget that the higher your child climbs in his sport then the greater will become your responsibility and involvement.

It must also be stated right at the outset that it is the child who should urge his parents to take him swimming rather than the other way round. If the latter becomes the case then the outlook is bleak indeed.

As parents your most active help will be required. You will have to help convey your child to and fro from training, sometimes in the early morning. You will on occasions have to convey your child to and from competition and this may even be a trip abroad. You will have to plan your holidays to the last detail to avoid clashing with important swimming galas.

Your active help in making sure your child obtains the maximum possible sleep will be required. The mother should make her contribution the supervising of the child's eating habits, making sure that the young athlete has a varied, well-balanced diet at all times, including all necessary vitamins and keeping a check on weight, particularly of girls. Some swimmers will have to do their own mobility and circuit exercises at home and here the parents must maintain a strong interest, making sure that not only are these carried out but also that they are progressive in intensity according to the coach's instructions.

Your strong encouragement for your child will be required in particular when he does not swim well. Never try to criticize a poor performance; leave that to the coach whose job it is to advise and correct. Follow your child in competition—it is your duty to be there if possible—but never stay to watch the training. It should be one of our aims in all spheres of life to remember that *constructive* criticism is more likely to be accepted.

Never delay in discussing with your child's coach any problem on which you may require advice: the more difficult the problem then the speedier should liaison be established. I am sure all coaches welcome speedy, frank, open discussions as soon as possible after any problems arise.

The last thing parents should do when they have a problem of any sort on their minds is to sit back and say nothing. Ultimately the problem will snowball, becoming larger and larger until it may become impossible at a later date to resolve amicably.

When you decide to put your child's training into the hands of a coach, then from that moment on you owe it to that coach to consult him and no other for advice on any qualms or worries you may have about your child's swimming. If your child is not progressing as you feel he should be, then obtain even closer liaison with your coach until matters are sorted out.

Every coach and swimmer has a swimming relationship of some sort. Where the coach serves a large club or squad, then such relationships may be fairly distant, although the coach should try to be impartial and treat all his swimmers in identical manner without showing favouritism. Where the coach controls just a few swimmers, then the swimmer/coach relationship may become much more personal.

Again, I am sure I speak for all coaches when I say that if a coach realizes that for some reason there is a lack of harmony between himself and a swimmer, then he should be the first to approach and discuss such things with the parents. He should also realize that if the differences are great enough he should go to the extent of advising a change of coach, which as a last resort he should certainly be big enough to do.

Another very useful job which parents can do is to help, encourage and assist their child to keep a written record of all his training times and competition times. It is a long hard road to the top and, no matter how dedicated a swimmer may be, there will always be occasions when a fall-off in performance may cause temporary lack of interest. This is when parents can help by looking up past performances and training times to stimulate new interest.

Parents can also help by keeping up to date with swimming advertisements regarding forthcoming galas, etc. Not many clubs have absolutely full competitive programmes and your child may well like to go a little farther afield to obtain better competition. Parents with just a little ingenuity can make suitable medal shields on which children's awards can be mounted. Such things as this will help sustain and stimulate active interest as well as provide a record of memorable times past when swimming careers end.

Another way in which parents can help their child is to start a swimming scrap-book of the events surrounding the club or the individual, especially if the child features in local press reports on his own swimming; it all encourages the build-up required for success.

Finally, as parents of swimmers, always remember when some journey or task in connection with your child's swimming seems particularly irksome that some parents have actually emigrated to other countries solely to provide their children with what they consider the very best in training facilities for their sport.